Autism
Spectrum
Disorder

Autism Spectrum Disorder

A CLINICAL GUIDE FOR GENERAL PRACTITIONERS

V. MARK DURAND

American Psychological Association • Washington, DC

Published by
American Psychological Association
750 First Street, NE
Washington, DC 20002
www.apa.org

To order
APA Order Department
P.O. Box 92984
Washington, DC 20090-2984
Tel: (800) 374-2721; Direct: (202) 336-5510
Fax: (202) 336-5502; TDD/TTY: (202) 336-6123
Online: www.apa.org/pubs/books
E-mail: order@apa.org

In the U.K., Europe, Africa, and the Middle East, copies may be ordered from
American Psychological Association
3 Henrietta Street
Covent Garden, London
WC2E 8LU England

Typeset in Minion by Circle Graphics, Inc., Columbia, MD

Printer: Maple Press, York, PA
Cover Designer: Mercury Publishing Services, Rockville, MD

The opinions and statements published are the responsibility of the authors, and such opinions and statements do not necessarily represent the policies of the American Psychological Association.

Library of Congress Cataloging-in-Publication Data
Durand, Vincent Mark.
  Autism spectrum disorder : a clinical guide for general practitioners / by V. Mark Durand.
    pages cm
  Includes bibliographical references and index.
  ISBN 978-1-4338-1569-0 — ISBN 1-4338-1569-9 1. Autism spectrum disorders.
2. Autism spectrum disorders in children. 3. Evidence-based medicine. I. Title.
  RC553.A88D86 2014
  616.85'882—dc23
                           2013017833

British Library Cataloguing-in-Publication Data
A CIP record is available from the British Library.

Printed in the United States of America
First Edition

http://dx.doi.org/10.1037/14283-000

To Wendy, my love for over three decades and my constant inspiration.
—*V. Mark Durand*

Contents

Acknowledgments

I would like to acknowledge some of the many individuals who have taught me about autism spectrum disorder (ASD) and who served as models for the ideal scientist–practitioner. First and foremost, I must express my gratitude to the numerous individuals with ASD along with their families, teachers, and other caregivers who have taught me so much about this enigmatic disorder. I am especially grateful to the family members who have been so open with their many joys and challenges; their accounts have helped guide my own professional growth and have informed my research for the last three decades.

My first exposure to this population was in the experimental school at Binghamton University under the guidance of Ray Romanczyk; I thank him for introducing me to all of the children and families who courageously fought for the best care. My colleagues there—especially Dan Crimmins and Debbie Hoffman-Plotkin—also served as incredible role models for clinical competence and personal compassion. My subsequent work with the late Edward (Ted) Carr cemented my interest in this field, and I owe him an incredible debt of gratitude for 22 years as a mentor and as a friend. Many individuals in our field are outstanding exemplars of care and professionalism, and I thank them all.

I would like to thank the students in my Autism Spectrum Disorder class for reading drafts of the chapters and providing feedback. I would like to thank Susan Reynolds at the American Psychological Association (APA) for her support and encouragement throughout this project, APA development editor Susan Herman, and two anonymous reviewers who were extremely helpful to me by "filling in the holes" and making terrific suggestions for making the manuscript that much better. Finally, I am indebted to Ashley Smith and Marly Sadou at the University of South Florida St. Petersburg, who helped on many different aspects of the research and writing of this book. Their intellect and perseverance assisted me beyond my expectations, and am I deeply grateful to them both.

Autism Spectrum Disorder

Introduction

My experience with persons having autism spectrum disorder (ASD) spans 4 decades. In the early days, saying that I worked with autistic children was likely to trigger a response such as "That's great that you have an interest in helping children with their art!" Today, you would be hard-pressed to find an informed adult who was not somewhat aware of autism, and many know someone affected. Because of the frequent media coverage, most are also aware that there has been an alarming increase in persons diagnosed with ASD. For example, the Centers for Disease Control and Prevention estimated that one in 50 school-age children has received a diagnosis that falls within the category of ASD (Blumberg, Bramlett, Kogan, Schieve, & Jones, 2013); a growing number of adults are being diagnosed with ASD as well.

As a consequence of the rising numbers of persons identified as having ASD, clinicians are increasingly presented with clients who may fall

http://dx.doi.org/10.1037/14283-007
Autism Spectrum Disorder: A Clinical Guide for General Practitioners, by V. M. Durand

on the autism spectrum or who have a family member affected by some form of this disorder. However, many clinicians are not formally trained to deal with these types of specific and significant problems. My colleagues and I receive constant referrals by clinicians who recognize that some of the persons with ASD present challenges outside their area of expertise. However, there are also times when clinicians are appropriately trained either to intervene with an individual on the higher end of the spectrum or to assist family and friends of the affected individual. The goal of this guide is to help clinicians make these important distinctions.

When faced with clients who challenge one's boundaries of competence, it is clearly important to know when one's skills and background may be limited and when outside consultation or expertise is required. This guide is designed to help clinicians adhere to American Psychological Association (2010) Ethical Standard 2.01: Boundaries of Competence:

> (a) Psychologists provide services, teach, and conduct research with populations and in areas only within the boundaries of their competence, based on their education, training, supervised experience, consultation, study, or professional experience. (p. 4)

In addition to addressing the needs of clinicians with no formal training or experience with clients on the autism spectrum, the information in this book may also be of value to individuals who do have an applied background in ASD. There has been an explosion of new research on ASD (G. Dawson, 2013). Unfortunately, the rapidly expanding knowledge base in this field has not been easily accessible to the individuals working in this field. New discoveries in genetics (explaining why one could have a child with ASD without a family history of the disorder), neurobiology (e.g., the role of paternal age on ASD), development (new work showing the different trajectories of the disorder), treatment (numerous randomized clinical trials since 2011), and even our understanding about how early intensive behavioral intervention affects brain development have revolutionized our understanding of the spectrum of disorders. For example, I discuss how current research on the early development of the social brain in persons with ASD can help explain why teaching communication skills for requests (e.g., "Can I have a cookie?") is much easier than teaching social communication skills (e.g., "Hello, how are you?"), and I consider the implications these differences have for intervention approaches. It is clear that there is an urgent need to communicate these developments in a way that can be useful to clinicians.

The goal for this book is not to provide sufficient information to be able to properly assess and treat all individuals. Rather, the objective is to provide background on ASD and outline decision points that help clarify when a clinician has the requisite skills to help and when a referral to a specialist is needed. The type of specialized assistance needed is suggested on the basis of current knowledge of evidence-based assessments and treatments. Several clinical cases are described and used throughout the chapters to bring to life these disorders and appropriate approaches to their assessment and treatment.

CLINICAL CONCERNS

This book includes highlighted *clinical concerns*—important issues that clinicians are likely to face when assessing and treating people with ASD and their families. For example, the section on genetics calls attention to the frequently voiced concern of parents: "If I have another child, what's the likelihood that this child will have an ASD?" Another issue concerns IQ tests: The lack of social motivation (characteristic of persons with ASD) can skew the results of some IQ tests because social motivation (e.g., wanting to please a parent or teacher with test performance) is low or absent in this group. I hope that these discussions prepare clinicians for these and other difficult issues they will encounter when working with this population.

LANGUAGE

The language used throughout this guide is important to note. Although the changes in the fifth edition of the *Diagnostic and Statistical Manual of Mental Disorders* (*DSM–5;* American Psychiatric Association, 2013) eliminated the distinction between persons in need of extensive supports, as described by Leo Kanner, and those who are verbal and need fewer supports, as described by Hans Asperger (i.e., the condition previously referred to as *Asperger's disorder*), there is still a need to highlight these distinctions. I use nonstandard labels such as *Kanner's type ASD* and *Asperger's type ASD* to help clarify these distinctions where they are needed. In addition, I use person-first language to refer to individuals with ASD in order to recognize that people are more than their disorders. Therefore, the term *autistic child* and related language are replaced with *a child with autism* or *a person with ASD*. In most areas of psychopathology this is becoming standard, and there is little controversy over this convention. However, as will be seen, it is not a simple matter in the field of ASD. Some individuals with the disorder prefer to refer to themselves with terms like *autistics* or *Aspies* (persons previously diagnosed with Asperger's disorder) and are offended by attempts to separate the label from their own identity (Pellicano & Stears, 2011). No consensus has emerged regarding the most acceptable terminology. Additionally, the book uses the term *disorder* in keeping with the terminology of the *DSM–5* and the 10th edition of the *International Classification of Diseases* (*ICD–10;* World Health Organization, 1993). I acknowledge, however, that there are legitimate arguments by some with ASD that this condition is not a psychological or mental health disorder but a different (and perhaps superior) way of viewing the world (Mottron, 2011). These controversies are discussed in later chapters.

Several other complications in the use of terminology require explanation. The spectrum of autism-related disorders is wide and includes individuals who have no functional communication skills and others who can carry on sophisticated conversations. Similarly, the ability to interact with others varies as widely as do intellectual abilities among these individuals. As a result, the phrases *high functioning* and *low functioning* are sometimes used to distinguish persons on either end of this spectrum. This distinction is not based on any quantitative criteria and is typically used as a convenience. The exception is the use of the label *high functioning autism* to identify a group of individuals who have better communication and social skills as well as average or above-average cognitive abilities. It remains unclear whether this group is a distinct subgroup that can be distinguished from those who previously received the diagnosis of Asperger's disorder (Calzada, Pistrang, & Mandy, 2012).

Finally, I avoid the term *normal* and instead use the term *typical,* which is the convention used in the ASD field. For example, I use the phrase "a typically developing child" to describe a child who might otherwise be described as developing normally. This is to avoid making judgments about what might be considered "abnormal." Again, there continues to be substantial sensitivity to the use of labels among those in the ASD community, and clinicians should be aware of potentially offending these individuals and their families.

ORGANIZATION OF THE BOOK

The structure of this book follows the different areas of knowledge that are important when aiding persons with ASD and their families. In Chapter 1, I describe the historical contexts for the current understanding of the different types of ASD, including individuals with classic "autism" as well as those on the other end of the autism spectrum such as the Asperger's type of ASD. I introduce two cases representing these two extremes and refer to them throughout the book to put a face on how concerns such as assessment and treatment are addressed.[1] Chapter 2 looks at the current diagnostic criteria for *DSM–5* and *ICD–10* and describes the changes and controversies introduced by the modifications made in *DSM–5*. Chapter 3 abstracts the current state of knowledge as to what genetic, neurobiological, and environmental factors may conspire to result in these profound social and communicative differences. Chapter 4 points out conditions and problems commonly associated with ASD including intellectual disability, obsessive–compulsive disorder, anxiety, gastrointestinal problems, and sleeping difficulties. Chapters 5 and 6 cover more applied concerns, such as screening, diagnosis and assessment, and treatment. Chapter 7,

---

[1]Details of the cases have been altered to protect clients' confidentiality.

which addresses the needs of family members, describes research on an approach that combines cognitive behavior therapy with behavioral parent training to significantly improve outcomes both for parents and their children. Emphasized throughout are decision points at which clinicians can decide when to intervene directly and when to refer clients elsewhere for evidence-based assistance.

1

Autism Spectrum Disorder: Background and Cases

Autism spectrum disorder (ASD) is a neurodevelopmental disorder that, at its core, affects how one perceives and socializes with others. In other words, the very essence of our social universe that we take for granted each day—smiling at a friend, sympathetically reaching out to touch the hand of someone in distress, or recognizing from a loved one's tone of voice that there is a problem—is seriously impaired or completely absent in persons affected by ASD. In addition, for people with this disorder, the nature of their communication is affected, and they share a propensity to display highly restricted and often disruptive behaviors. At times their reactions seem to defy the accepted laws of behavior we have come to take for granted (e.g., hitting oneself even though this produces pain). ASD is clearly neurologically based, and there is an extensive research literature that focuses on the underlying genetic and neurobiological underpinnings of this condition (Amaral, Dawson, & Geschwind, 2011).

http://dx.doi.org/10.1037/14283-008
Autism Spectrum Disorder: A Clinical Guide for General Practitioners, by V. M. Durand

More and more clinicians are presented with clients who either have ASD or whose lives are affected by this enigmatic disorder. Whether the client displays comorbid difficulties or faces situations that can complicate treatment and outcomes (e.g., marital or family challenges), these special circumstances can test the skills of even the most experienced and broadly trained clinician. This guide describes the range and severity of ASD symptoms and offers suggestions for diagnosis, assessment, and treatment. To understand the current thinking and controversies surrounding ASD, it is useful to first describe the background of how this disorder was discovered.

HISTORICAL CONTEXT

It has been approximately seven decades since noted psychiatrist Leo Kanner (1943) described 11 children whose development and behavior were so strikingly different from other typically developing children, including "autistic aloneness" (taken from the Greek word *auto* meaning self as a reference to their extreme social deficits) and "insistence on sameness." (These characteristics are comparable to the description in the fifth edition of the *Diagnostic and Statistical Manual of Mental Disorders (DSM–5);* American Psychiatric Association, 2013: "restricted, repetitive patterns of behavior, interests, or activities"; p. 50.) Kanner hypothesized that the children were born without the usual motivation for social interaction, a concept that plays a major role in understanding the social, communicative, and behavioral differences observed in these individuals (S. Goldstein & Ozonoff, 2008). This type of ASD (sometimes referred to as *autism, classic autism,* or *Kanner's autism*) often presents as an apparent disinterest in others (social impairment), delayed language development, and restricted and repetitive patterns of behavior (e.g., interest in lining things up and great displeasure if thwarted from doing so).

At around the same time that Kanner (1943) identified the puzzling behavior of a group of children he discussed in his article "Autistic Disturbances of Affective Contact," Austrian physician Hans Asperger described four children with "autistic psychopathy" (Asperger, 1944/1991; Frith, 1991), or a difficulty relating to other children. In contrast to Kanner's children, this group appeared to be intact intellectually (Klin, 2011). These children had difficulty in school because of their behavioral outbursts in situations with others. They appeared to lack the ability to understand why others did not behave in ways they wanted; they were greatly upset by such behavior.

As these two types of disorders characterized by marked social impairments were being delineated, it was also noticed that, unlike classic autism that seemed to be present from birth, other children displayed typical development for the first years of life, followed by a loss of social and communication skills. Described by Theodore Heller and later labeled *childhood disintegrative disorder,* these children ultimately appeared very similar to the children described by Kanner despite their early typical development (Rutter, Bailey, Bolton, & Couteur, 1994; Volkmar, Klin, Schultz, & State, 2009).

The fourth revised text edition of the *Diagnostic and Statistical Manual of Mental Disorders* (American Psychiatric Association, 2000) included the three disorders just described (autistic disorder, Asperger's disorder, and childhood disintegrative disorder) under the general category of *pervasive developmental disorders.* Also included in the manual are two other disorders: Rett's disorder, a progressive neurodegenerative disorder that is almost exclusively observed in females and is characterized by constant hand-wringing, intellectual disability, and impaired motor skills (Kaufmann et al., 2012; Neul et al., 2010); and pervasive developmental disorder not otherwise specified (PDDNOS), a category used to describe those who had some of the features of classic autism but did not fulfill all of the criteria. In the *DSM–5,* neither Rett's disorder nor PDDNOS is considered in the category of ASD. Some of the disorders previously considered under the heading of pervasive developmental disorders (autistic disorder, Asperger's disorder, and childhood disintegrative disorder) are now classified in the *DSM–5* as part of a spectrum of disorders (autism spectrum disorder), a group of disorders that are thought to be related through the sharing of risk genes or pathophysiological mechanisms (S. E. Hyman, 2007). This is an explicit recognition that these disorders share common social communication deficits and repetitive and restricted behaviors and that they may represent one underlying condition. Finally, *DSM–5* now includes a new disorder (social communication disorder) that includes the difficulties in social communication seen in ASD but without restricted, repetitive patterns of behavior. Some individuals previously diagnosed with PDDNOS may fall into this category.

In the following section, two cases are presented to illustrate the spectrum of difficulties faced by persons with divergent forms of ASD.

CLINICAL CASES

The first case describes a child with a severe form of ASD (previously referred to as *autistic disorder*) and focuses on the effects such a child can have on members of the family. The second case describes a young man with what was previously diagnosed as Asperger's disorder (now classified as a type of "high functioning" ASD) who might be typical of an individual presenting to a clinician for comorbid problems. These cases are referred to throughout the book.

Selena, Jorge, and Daughter Maria

Selena and Jorge were in their mid-20s when they married. Both had come from large families, and they were looking forward to starting a family of their own. Selena was a manager for a chain of jewelry stores and had a reputation for turning around underperforming groups. Jorge worked in construction, and his work opportunities were sporadic. In economic declines he would go for weeks and sometimes months without employment. There had been some issues between them about their disparate salaries, but each seemed to handle this well until their first child was born. Their beautiful infant, Maria, was their dream come true, although she could be a handful. She was a fussy baby who had a difficult time breastfeeding and by 12 months still did not go to bed or sleep through the night without crying. Her parents had some concerns but were initially told that Maria would probably "grow out of" the problems they were seeing. She seemed fine physically and did well in her early tests of motor skills and development.

At Maria's 18-month checkup her pediatrician suspected that she might be delayed in her social development and recommended further assessment. A developmental pediatrician performed a comprehensive screening and noted that despite her typical development on physical milestones (fine and gross motor skills), she was delayed in her cognitive, language, and social skills. Most notably, Maria did not display "shared attention" (e.g., looking back and forth between a favorite toy and her parents), did not point and look at someone to get something she wanted, and still had no spoken words. Her parents reported that she loved to line things up, such as toys or silverware, and she would become extremely upset if these objects were touched or put away. She also seemed to enjoy jumping up and down and flapping her hands, which they interpreted as a sign that she was happy and excited. The preliminary diagnosis of ASD (at the time labeled *autistic disorder*) was shocking to her parents, who felt that they might have contributed to her problems.

Selena initially presented to a therapist complaining of symptoms of depression and anxiety. She had recently had an apparent panic attack in a supermarket, which frightened her; she sought medical treatment, and when no medical cause was found, she was referred to a therapist. As she described her concerns it was clear that the stresses of having a difficult child and a demanding job were taking a toll on Selena and her relationship with Jorge. The couple often fought about household chores and child rearing. Selena thought that because Jorge was unemployed for weeks at a time, he should be taking on a larger role at home during these periods. However, she felt that her husband was not stepping up, and she was overwhelmed that she was responsible for bringing in a stable income as well as being responsible for most household decisions. Adding to this stress was Maria's recent diagnosis of ASD. Selena especially felt guilty that she did not spend enough time with Maria because of her job, and these thoughts contributed to her anxiety and depression.

Throughout the book, I revisit the cases of Selena and Jorge, with special attention to the cognitive assessment of Selena's thoughts and feelings regarding herself, her husband, and Maria. In the final chapter, I describe an adaptation of cognitive behavior therapy that was used to help with her child-rearing concerns and evolving anxiety issues. The goal is to demonstrate how clinicians can address the specific and perhaps unique needs of parents such as Selena and Jorge.

Jacob

When 25-year-old Jacob first discussed his concerns with his therapist, the presenting problems were described as social anxiety and depressive symptoms. Jacob talked about being depressed, in part because he never had a girlfriend, and he wanted help learning how to speak with women. The clinician noted that Jacob was very verbal, although at times very formal in his use of words. He also appeared clear and focused in his thoughts. However, a short time into the initial interview, Jacob brought up his interest in the *Star Wars* movies. As he spoke about this fascination, his affect changed from the concerned look he displayed when discussing his problems to a bright and more animated demeanor. Jacob's enthusiasm for *Star Wars* was such that several times the therapist had to interrupt and return him to his purported history of depression and his previous relationships. Unfortunately, Jacob had little insight into his difficulties and also did not seem to pick up on his therapist's growing impatience with his inability to focus in the session.

As his therapist considered Jacob's difficulty staying focused (and wondered whether he had attention-deficit/hyperactivity disorder), he began to notice Jacob's unusual finger movements. He would from time to time pull back the fingers on his right hand and sometimes flick them in unusual ways. These strange hand gestures increased in frequency when Jacob excitedly turned the discussion back to *Star Wars*. Jacob seemed unaware that he was doing this with his fingers, and at times would slightly rock back and forth in his chair.

When the therapist could get Jacob to discuss his depression and concerns about relationships, Jacob appeared to want very practical solutions. "I want to expand my verbal repertoire to be able to express my thoughts to girls. If I tell a girl that she is attractive or I comment on a part of her anatomy as a means of complimenting her, that often leads to an unpleasant situation." His therapist, while noting the rather formal language Jacob used, followed up on his comment. "So, give me an example of the last time you talked to a young woman. Where were you?" "Well, yesterday I was in the library and there was a girl working on her laptop computer. It was the new line of thin laptops." Jacob proceeded to go into detail about the computer the young woman was using. "What did you do and say?" the therapist pressed. "I approached her and told her she had nice legs." "And what did she do?" The therapist guessed it didn't go well. "She told me to leave her alone. But she had pretty legs. What should I have said?" Jacob's naïveté about this encounter was surprising, and the therapist was taken aback.

Jacob spoke of his depression, sometimes using clinical jargon, but he had difficulty describing his feelings. He said his eating and sleeping habits had not changed markedly and that his main interest (*Star Wars*) still made him excited. Despite his reports of being depressed, Jacob showed few outward signs. In probing this concern about depression, he relayed that it was his mother who suggested he see the therapist and that he might be depressed:

> She always tells me to go out more. She doesn't like it that I collect so much *Star Wars* paraphernalia and watch the movies. She thinks I need to establish more personal relationships with members of the opposite sex and that I'm depressed.

When asked by his therapist why his mother thought he might be depressed, Jacob had no explanation. (Discrepancies in reports of depression between the parents and the child with ASD are common; see, e.g., Butzer & Konstantareas, 2003.)

In subsequent chapters, the case of Jacob is revisited to see how the therapist assessed his problems and ultimately helped him with his social skills problems.

These two clinical cases illustrate the range of developmental disorders common in ASD (from the more severe impairments displayed by Maria to the high functioning end as seen with Jacob) as well as the impact such a disorder can have on the person's family. The next chapter describes the characteristics of this disorder, including current thinking about the diagnostic criteria for ASD, and briefly covers the epidemiology of this disorder.

2

Diagnostic Criteria
and Epidemiology

This chapter highlights the diagnostic criteria for autism spectrum disorder (ASD) as delineated in the fifth edition of the *Diagnostic and Statistical Manual of Mental Disorders* (*DSM–5*; American Psychiatric Association, 2013) and provides a detailed description of the variety of manifestations of this disorder. The criteria in the *DSM–5* are compared with the criteria in the previous version of the manual (fourth ed., text revision; *DSM–IV–TR*; American Psychiatric Association, 2000) and the current criteria in the *International Classification of Diseases* (10th ed.; *ICD–10*; World Health Organization, 1993).[1] The goal of this chapter is to assist clinicians with identifying undiagnosed problems and to provide insight into the range of challenges faced by persons with ASD and those who live with them.

---

[1] The 11th edition of the *ICD* is expected to be published in 2015 (http://www.who.int/classifications/icd/revision/en/).

http://dx.doi.org/10.1037/14283-001
Autism Spectrum Disorder: A Clinical Guide for General Practitioners, by V. M. Durand

CHARACTERISTICS OF ASD

Two major characteristics of ASD are expressed in *DSM–5:* (a) impairments in social communication and social interaction; and (b) restricted behavior, interests, and activities (American Psychiatric Association, 2013). In addition, *DSM–5* recognizes that the impairments are present in early childhood and that they limit daily functioning. It is the degree of impairment in each of these characteristics that presumably distinguishes individuals previously diagnosed with the separate disorders of autistic disorder, Asperger's disorder, and pervasive developmental disorder not otherwise specified.

In *DSM–5*, the singular term *disorder* is used in the label *autism spectrum disorder* to suggest that the shared symptoms represent one core problem. This combination under one label remains controversial (McPartland, Reichow, & Volkmar, 2012). To meet the inclusion criteria for ASD, individuals must exhibit two symptom clusters, they must have limited and impaired ability to successfully function in a social world, and these symptoms must be evident early in life. (Note that these criteria are paraphrased; readers should refer to *DSM–5* for the exact wording.)

1. Continuing problems with social communication and interactions with others that are not primarily the result of significant developmental delays. All three of the following aspects of these problems must be observed.
    a. Difficulties with social reciprocity: These include the inability to successfully share interests or conversations in a typical back-and-forth manner.
    b. Difficulties with nonverbal communication: These can range from poor or absent eye contact to the lack of understanding of how nonverbal communication (e.g., a gesture, a facial expression) is used to fully communicate with others.
    c. Difficulties in creating or maintaining relationships with others: These can include a complete absence of interest in others and the inability to adjust to social situations enough to make friends.

2. Restricted and repetitive patterns of behavior, interests, or activities with at least two of the following patterns.

   a. Speech, motor movements, and/or use of objects that are overly stereotyped or repetitive.

   b. Disproportionate following of routines, repetitive patterns of verbal or nonverbal behavior, or extreme resistance to change.

   c. Extraordinarily strong fixations on objects or certain topics.

   d. Unusual responses to sensory input, including the apparent absence of usual responses or hyperresponsiveness to things such as loud noises, textures, smells, or lights.

As with all *DSM–5* disorders, the extent of the differences in behavior in ASD must rise to the level of limiting and impairing the ability of the person to function successfully in society. This is a defining characteristic of ASD. There has been a tendency to consider individuals who are bright but socially awkward as having ASD; some have speculated that Bill Gates and Albert Einstein fall on the spectrum. Clinicians need to be particularly cautious with individuals who self-diagnose with this disorder.

Problems With Social Communication and Interaction

Successful communication requires fairly sophisticated and developed nonverbal and sometimes (but not always) verbal abilities. It is an important social act. It is not surprising, then, that research on the communication and social abilities of individuals with ASD suggests considerable overlap between the two (Frazier et al., 2012; Gotham, Risi, Pickles, & Lord, 2007). Communication and social abilities were listed independently in *DSM–IV–TR;* they are part of the *ICD–10* criteria. *DSM–5* combines these two areas into one general symptom cluster: social communication/ interaction. Difficulties with social communication and interaction are further defined by the inclusion of three aspects—problems with social reciprocity, nonverbal communication, and initiating and maintaining social relationships—all of which must be present for a diagnosis of ASD to be made.

Social Reciprocity

Consider the following moments from daily life:

- You and another person reach for a door handle at the same time. You make eye contact, and perhaps the two of you exchange smiles; you let the other person go through first. Even if no words were uttered, you both shared a humorous moment.
- A little girl sees a toy she likes. She smiles, looks at her mother, looks back at the toy, and then looks back at her mother. Both mother and daughter understand: The little girl likes that toy, and they both enjoy the social interaction.
- You sit with an old friend and share stories about the good old days.

These scenarios are examples of *social reciprocity,* that is, sharing interests or conversation in a back-and-forth manner. This ability is either absent or impaired in persons with ASD. In the case of Maria, the young daughter of Selena and Jorge (presented in Chapter 1), one of the first signs that alerted the developmental pediatrician to a problem was Maria's lack of shared attention. She would not look back and forth between something she wanted and her parents as a way to communicate that she liked and wanted something. In fact, her parents reported that instead she might take their hand and use it almost as a tool to get something she wanted. For young children with ASD, this lack of shared or joint attention is a major developmental signal that social reciprocity is impaired (Gillespie-Lynch et al., 2012; Schietecatte, Roeyers, & Warreyn, 2012).

On the other end of the spectrum, 25-year-old Jacob (also introduced in Chapter 1) displayed difficulties with social reciprocity. In his case, however, the problem was more subtle. He could express an interest (e.g., liking a young woman's legs), but he had a limited understanding of how his communication would affect the other person (e.g., annoy or insult her). For instance, he could not interpret from the expression on another person's face how his words were being received. Not understanding that things he would say might create a negative reaction in others interfered with his ability to sustain conversations. Constantly talking about *Star Wars* and not attending to the other person's interests tended to push people away from him, but he was not able to recognize this. Jacob lacked what is referred to as *theory of mind*, or the ability to infer what others might be thinking or feeling (Baron-Cohen, Tager-Flusberg, & Cohen, 2000). We rely on our attempts to "read other people's minds" in order to maintain social interactions. If you are talking to someone who continues to look at her watch, you will likely try to guess what she is thinking (e.g., she's bored with the conversation, she's expecting a phone call). We use this skill to navigate conversations and manage social interactions (perhaps trying to wrap up the discussion or switch topics). However, in Jacob and others with ASD, this ability is impaired and therefore results in problems with social reciprocity.

Nonverbal Communication

Have you ever been cornered by a person who stands too close to you while talking? This simple nonverbal action—misestimating social distance—can negatively affect a simple interaction. Again, in ASD these types of nonverbal behaviors, such as properly estimating social distance, gestures, or eye contact, are often problematic and are usually apparent by the age of 12 months (Rozga et al., 2011). For example, the 18-month-old Maria would not make eye contact with other people (including her parents) when they spoke to her. Other children with ASD may look in the direction of the person speaking, but the impression is that they are looking through the speaker and not at him or her. They might smile or laugh without any obvious reason.

We take for granted our ability to make proper eye contact with others as part of social exchanges. When others speak to us, we tend to make constant eye contact. In fact, frequently looking away as someone tries to engage with us is usually interpreted as a sign of indifference and may be judged as rude. Yet, staring at someone without ever looking away can make the listener uncomfortable. This subtle nonverbal skill is learned early on in life, and when it is absent or disrupted it can make simple conversations uncomfortable.

Jacob would make eye contact with others as he spoke, although he would often look around and seem distracted as other people spoke to him. To observe him engage in conversation with another person, one had the impression that he was just waiting for the other person to stop speaking so he could go back to a topic of his interest. His therapist reported that he never felt Jacob was listening to him (a common feature in this range of ASD; Begeer, Bernstein, van Wijhe, Scheeren, & Koot, 2012) or that he was having a conversation; rather, it seemed only that two people were speaking in the same social space. Others with this level of ASD may lack appropriate facial expressions or tone of voice (also known as *prosody;* see McCann & Peppé, 2003; Paul, Augustyn, Klin, & Volkmar, 2005; Shriberg et al., 2001) when speaking or just give the appearance of general nonverbal awkwardness. Again, they often are not aware that their affect or nonverbal behavior is not socially appropriate in specific situations (e.g., laughing or talking to themselves while sitting in a doctor's waiting room).

Difficulties Creating or Maintaining Relationships With Others

The two previous symptom clusters (problems with social reciprocity and nonverbal communication) obviously can contribute to the inability to create new relationships or maintain current ones. Again, there is a broad range of these difficulties. As described in Chapter 1, Maria showed no interest in establishing relationships with other children. Her parents began to notice that other children her age would show more interest in children than adults when they were out in public, for example, shopping in the mall. However, their daughter did not seem to even notice other children but instead might fixate on a toy or some other object that she would come across in a store. Some individuals with ASD appear to have very little interest in other people other than as a means to an end (e.g., getting a favorite toy that is out of reach). They may smile and seem to want to be around others (e.g., sitting on a parent's lap), but this behavior is fleeting and inconsistent, making a "relationship" much more limited in nature.

On the other end of the autism spectrum, individuals may express interest in having relationships with others, but their social difficulties interfere with their desires (Orsmond, Krauss, & Seltzer, 2004). For example, Jacob had no insight into how his reaction to conversations with others might distance him from them. As his therapist noted, although he expressed interest in getting to know other people, his egocentric appearance (e.g., not showing any interest in listening to others unless they were discussing his favorite topics) could be interpreted as rudeness and certainly did not facilitate continued interactions. In addition, Jacob had a great deal of difficulty knowing the right and wrong things to say (as demonstrated by his personal remark to a total stranger that she had nice legs) and did not understand why some things he said might upset others. All of these social skills difficulties hampered his ability to maintain meaningful social relationships.

Restricted and Repetitive Patterns of Behavior, Interests, or Activities

Persons with ASD display behaviors that are relatively rigid or unusual (Leekam, Prior, & Uljarevic, 2011). These can sometimes extend to compulsive preoccupations with certain topics or activities. *DSM–5* defines this second aspect of ASD as including at least two of the patterns of behaviors described in this section. It is important to note that the first characteristics described in the first three subsections appear to include similar behaviors and therefore have significant overlap. For example, if someone enjoys lining up toys in a certain way and gets upset if they are moved from their preferred positions, this pattern of behavior seems to fulfill all three of those requirements. It is hoped that this will be clarified in future criteria under the heading of "restricted and repetitive patterns of behavior, interests, or activities."

Overly Stereotyped or Repetitive Speech, Motor Movements, or Use of Objects

In the first case study in Chapter 1, Maria's parents described how she loved to jump up and down excitedly when she was apparently happy; this behavior was always accompanied by repetitive hand flapping. She could do this for minutes at a time. Individuals with this type of classic autism sometimes spend hours spinning objects or picking up lint and watching it fall to the ground without losing interest; some individuals will repeat words or phrases over and over again (echolalia; Durand, 2011b). These types of behaviors sometimes appear to be in reaction to some emotional situation (e.g., appearing happy or anxious), and at other times they seem to be independent of any external events and appear to be just part of the individual's inner world.

Jacob engaged in discrete hand movements when he was talking to his therapist (e.g., bending his fingers back in a repetitive way) and at times rocked back and forth in his chair when excited. The therapist later learned from Jacob's mother that he would sit and watch his *Star Wars* movies, often flapping his hands in a stereotyped way when he was excited. Jacob reported that he was usually unaware that he was doing this and had to work at controlling it in public. Some with this disorder will describe rocking back and forth or engaging in other types of repetitive behaviors as soothing to them (Grandin, 2011).

Disproportionate Following of Routines, Repetitive Patterns of Behavior, or Extreme Resistance to Change

Kanner (1943) described how the children he first identified as having "autistic disturbances of affective contact" had a strong preference for keeping some things or activities unbothered (what he called "insistence on sameness"). They might follow the same route to a store or touch every door as they walk down a hall; changes or interruptions to this routine might result in agitated or violent behavior. Others may ask the same question repeatedly or insist on having the same food or wearing the same clothes each day. Maria liked to line up toys or silverware and would have loud tantrums if items were moved. She would eat only macaroni and cheese for dinner and would become extremely agitated and refuse to eat if given anything else.

Jacob had rituals regarding his *Star Wars* materials. He constantly inventoried them in his room and could tell if anything was moved. If his room was disturbed in any way, he would become belligerent; it took a long time for him to eventually settle down. This excessive resistance to change and the resulting behavior problems are among the more distressing aspects of ASD, and family members are significantly affected. As I describe in Chapter 7, many families go to great lengths to avoid these types of confrontations and can end up figuratively and sometimes literally trapped in their own homes (Durand, 2011c).

Extraordinarily Strong Fixations on Objects or Topics

The restrictive and repetitive behaviors and interests cluster that is characteristic of ASD includes overlapping behaviors. Individuals with ASD focus on things or subjects that often become all consuming. Some children will need to carry a favorite object (e.g., a shoelace, a small toy) with them at all times. The difficulty comes into play when this is either not allowed because it is socially unacceptable (e.g., holding on to a toy in school during lessons) or when the object is misplaced. This behavior, like the rigid adherence to routines, can result in a great deal of disruption (e.g., tantrums, repeated requests for specific objects).

Many individuals with more functional skills will tend to fixate on a topic or topics (e.g., Jacob and his fascination with *Star Wars*). Although most people have favorite areas of interest (e.g., music, classic cars, photography), those with ASD are distinguished by the extent to which their interests dominate their lives. As described in the section on social communication difficulties, those with ASD have a single-minded fascination with a topic or topics, which results in their steering conversations back to these areas at the expense of the "give and take" usually found in conversation.

There are positive aspects to this laserlike focus on a particular topic. If their interests can be channeled correctly, those with ASD can take advantage of this trait. Temple Grandin (probably one of the most famous individuals with ASD today) had an interest in cattle and engineering; she earned a doctorate in animal husbandry and developed enclosures that helped move cows from place to place in more humane ways. Other fields require that researchers focus their attention on sometimes mundane or narrow topics, often for years or decades, and there are numerous examples of persons with ASD who have successfully taken advantage of their selective interests. Research on the cognitive skills of people with ASD (usually on the more advanced end of the autism spectrum) suggests that they may outperform persons without ASD on some visuospatial skills that require them to maintain attention on local information (Jolliffe &

Baron-Cohen, 1997; Pellicano, Maybery, Durkin, & Maley, 2006; Plaisted, O'Riordan, & Baron-Cohen, 1998).

Unusual Responses to Sensory Input

The addition of a consideration of the sensory issues observed in and sometimes reported by persons with ASD is new to *DSM–5* (Billstedt, Gillberg, & Gillberg, 2007; Leekam, Nieto, Libby, Wing, & Gould, 2007). Other diagnostic systems (e.g., *DSM–IV–TR, ICD–10*) made no mention of these symptoms as part of the identification of ASD (Wing, Gould, & Gillberg, 2011). Although not every person with ASD displays unusual responses to different sensory input, it is extremely common and (like the other types of restrictive and repetitive behaviors) very disruptive (Billstedt et al., 2007).

Maria's parents reported that she often appeared deaf when she was an infant; she did not respond to being called by her name and often did not respond even to very loud noises that would startle others. However, some individuals with ASD will become very agitated by loud noises or environments that are too dark or too bright. Interestingly, in an effort to address these problems, certain movie theaters offer "sensory friendly" showings of films for persons with ASD by employing strategies such as keeping the house lights on in the theater, reducing the volume, and allowing talking and the sometimes unusual noises made by some with ASD. Some individuals have fixations or aversions to certain smells and food textures that seem to contribute to their unusual and picky eating habits (see Chapter 4, this volume; see also Gaspar de Alba & Bodfish, 2011).

DIAGNOSTIC CRITERIA

The *DSM–IV–TR* identified ASD and other developmental disorders under the umbrella phrase *pervasive developmental disorders* (American Psychiatric Association, 2000). Individuals with pervasive developmental disorders experience problems with language, socialization, and cognition. The term *pervasive* was used to indicate that these problems are not relatively minor but significantly affect individuals throughout their lives.

Included under the heading of pervasive developmental disorders were autistic disorder (or autism), Asperger's disorder, Rett's disorder, childhood disintegrative disorder, and pervasive developmental disorder not otherwise specified (PDDNOS). These categories roughly map to the pervasive developmental disorders described in the *ICD–10* (World Health Organization, 1993). See Table 2.1.

In the *DSM–5*, most of these disorders are grouped under the label *autism spectrum disorder*. The rationale behind this reorganization of the separate autism-related disorders under one rubric was that they all share the pervasive deficits in social communication skills as well as the restricted patterns of behaviors. Within this category, however, there were considerable inconsistencies (Frazier et al., 2012; Rutter, 2011b). It was argued that the main differences among the disorders are ones involving the severity of the symptoms, language level, and levels of intellectual deficit. In *DSM–5*, Rett's disorder was deleted and, instead, persons with this disorder and other known genetic disorders that also have features of ASD (e.g., fragile X) will receive a diagnosis of ASD with the genetic disorders considered associated features (Lord & Jones, 2012).

Both Jacob and Maria had difficulties relating to others, and both had restricted patterns of behavior (Jacob's fixation on *Star Wars* and his finger and hand movements; Maria's interest in lining up objects and throwing severe tantrums when this was interrupted). According to the *DSM–5*, they would now receive the same diagnosis—ASD—with ratings on the severity of their other symptoms.

ASD LEVELS OF SEVERITY

To accommodate the range of difficulties in the two symptom clusters (social and communication interaction; restricted interests and repetitive behaviors), *DSM–5* introduced three levels of severity: Level 1, "Requiring support"; Level 2, "Requiring substantial support"; and Level 3, "Requiring very substantial support." Separate ratings are provided for social and communication interaction and for restricted interests and repetitive behaviors. This focus on levels of support is similar to the American Association on

Table 2.1

Comparison of Diagnostic Categories for Autism-Related Disorders

DSM–5	DSM–IV–TR	ICD–10
Neurodevelopmental disorders	Pervasive developmental disorders	Pervasive developmental disorders
A 09 Autism spectrum disorder (included with specification of severity of symptoms)	299.00 Autistic disorder	F84.0 Childhood autism
		F84.1 Atypical autism
Excluded	299.80 Rett's disorder	F84.2 Rett's syndrome
A 09 Autism spectrum disorder (included without reference to prior typical development)	299.10 Childhood disintegrative disorder	F84.3 Childhood disintegrative disorder
		F84.4 Overactive disorder associated with mental retardation and stereotyped movements
A 09 Autism spectrum disorder (included with specification of severity of symptoms)	299.80 Asperger's disorder	F84.5 Asperger's syndrome
		F84.8 Other pervasive developmental disorders
A 09 Autism spectrum disorder (included with specification of severity of symptoms)	299.80 Pervasive developmental disorder not otherwise specified (including atypical autism)	F84.9 Pervasive developmental disorders, unspecified

Note. DSM–5 = *Diagnostic and Statistical Manual of Mental Disorders* (5th ed.; American Psychiatric Association, 2013); DSM–IV–R = *Diagnostic and Statistical Manual of Mental Disorders* (4th ed., text revision; American Psychiatric Association, 2000); ICD–10 = *International Classification of Disease* (10th ed.; World Health Organization, 1993).

Intellectual and Developmental Disabilities' categorization of intellectual disability based on the level of support or assistance people need: intermittent, limited, extensive, or pervasive rather than on an IQ score (Thompson et al., 2009). Each level of support is described qualitatively and, as yet, has no quantitative equivalent. This makes assigning the appropriate level of support needed somewhat problematic if the person with ASD does not perform at the extreme ends of these categories (e.g., Maria at Level 3, Jacob at Level 1).

Levels of Severity for Social Communication Skills

Use of the levels of severity for social communication skills introduced into *DSM–5*'s diagnostic criteria is perhaps the best way to currently discriminate between the two extremes of the autism spectrum (see Figure 2.1). For example, Jacob could interact with others reasonably well if his mother was present to prompt him to stay on topic (i.e., with some supports). However, without these cues from another person, he

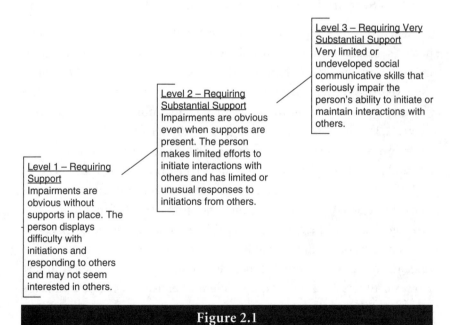

Figure 2.1

Levels of severity for social communication skills.

would fall back to his usual state of dominating conversations with his preoccupations, including *Star Wars,* placing him in the Level 1 category ("Requiring support"). Without support, his social communication skills were not sufficient to maintain significant social relationships with people outside of his immediate group of family members.

Maria's apparent disinterest in others except for how they could obtain things for her (e.g., a toy on a shelf, a cookie in a cabinet) placed her in the Level 3 range of social communication skills ("Requiring very substantial support"). Absent any major intervention to help her change her social motivation (which is described in the chapter on treatment), it is unlikely that she will develop significant social relationships with others.

It is relatively easy to assign a level of severity to those on the two extremes of the severity level continuum; those with a more mixed clinical picture will be difficult to categorize. Quantifying this type of rating will be a major goal for future diagnostic research.

Levels of Severity for Restricted Interests and Repetitive Behaviors

There does not appear to be a strong correlation between the level of a person's social communication abilities and the severity of their restricted interests and repetitive behaviors (Mandy & Skuse, 2008). In other words, the levels of severity for restricted interests and repetitive behaviors do not map consistently on the levels of social communication skills (see Figure 2.2). Those with the more classic Kanner's type ASD who have severely limited social skills may or may not have severely restricted interests and repetitive behaviors; the same is true for those on the Asperger's end of the spectrum. The levels of severity are determined by how pervasive these behaviors are, how much they impact daily functioning, and how vigorously the person resists being interrupted from these behaviors. Maria and Jacob would probably fall in the Level 2 range; they require substantial support in terms of their resistance to changing their routines. However, others can become quite violent when routines or behaviors are interrupted (including the display of significant aggression, tantrums, or self-injury), and this is true among individuals with a range of social communication skills (Durand & Merges, 2009; Wegner, 2012).

Level 3 – Requiring Very Substantial Support
The repetitive behaviors or ritualistic patterns seriously interfere with the person's ability to function successfully across contexts. The person is in obvious distress when others attempt to interrupt these behaviors and will struggle to return to them.

Level 2 – Requiring Substantial Support
The repetitive behaviors or ritualistic patterns occur across settings and are frequent enough to be readily observed by others. The person vigorously resists efforts to interrupt these repetitive behaviors or rituals.

Level 1 – Requiring Support
The repetitive behaviors or ritualistic patterns interfere with functioning in a limited number of settings. The person resists efforts to interrupt these repetitive behaviors or rituals.

Figure 2.2

Levels of severity for restricted and repetitive behaviors and interests.

OVERVIEW OF ASD DIAGNOSIS

DSM–5 modified the "autism triad" (deficits in social skills, deficits in communication, and restricted and repetitive behaviors and interests) that was previously assumed to be the core difficulties to include just the two behavior clusters (social communication skills difficulties and restricted behaviors). This reorganization will be a source of continued research in the coming years, especially as researchers search for biomarkers and brain mechanisms for these difficulties (Happé & Ronald, 2008). The addition of levels of severity is provided to guide clinicians and educators towards areas important for further assessment and treatment.

Early writings on ASD suggested that the social and communicative difficulties displayed by children with ASD were likely present from birth (Kanner, 1943). However, children are usually not identified until they are older because these distinctive behaviors are not readily apparent in very

---

Clinical Concerns: Asperger's Disorder as a Label

There is considerable controversy over the elimination of a separate category for Asperger's disorder in *DSM–5* (Baron-Cohen, 2009; Frances, 2010). In addition to questioning the scientific rationale for combining this disorder into the generic autism spectrum disorder, many in the community of persons who have been previously diagnosed with Asperger's disorder feel that this decision takes away part of their identity (Pellicano & Stears, 2011). Rather than feeling shame or embarrassment about receiving this diagnosis, many individuals embrace their distinctiveness. Some advocate for seeing these differences in terms of "neurodiversity" or viewing ASD as a different but not abnormal way to view the world (Armstrong, 2010; Singer, 1999). In fact, some individuals refer to themselves with pride as *Aspies* (e.g., Beardon & Worton, 2011), and those who do not have this disorder are sometimes pejoratively referred to as *neurotypical*. It is essential, therefore, to be sensitive when probing for how this cluster of symptoms may affect the individual with a diagnosis of ASD (Kapp, Gillespie-Lynch, Sherman, & Hutman, 2013).

---

young infants. At the same time, a second pattern of development was described in the case of those diagnosed with childhood disintegrative disorder. In these cases, children appeared to develop in a typical manner, but they later lost the social and communicative skills they once had and eventually came to resemble children with autism (Volkmar, 1992). This simple distinction is now being questioned, and research on children at-risk for ASD suggests that there may be a variety of developmental presentations (Ozonoff, Heung, Byrd, Hansen, & Hertz-Picciotto, 2008). In one prospective longitudinal study, researchers found that children later diagnosed as having ASD appeared to develop in parallel with their typical peers up to the age of 6 months in skills such as gaze to faces, shared smiles, and vocalizations to others (Ozonoff et al., 2010). After that age, varying patterns emerged, with some children beginning to lose those skills (regression) and others plateauing and regressing at a later age. Some work suggests that immune function changes in the brain affecting the amygdala (the area of the brain involved with fear and anxiety) may cause some regressive types of ASD (Breece et al., 2012). This type of work contributed to the *DSM–5*'s elimination of the later regression pattern as a distinct disorder (childhood disintegrative disorder). Although more work is needed in this area, what was previously believed about the course of ASD appears to be called into question (Lord, Luyster, Guthrie, & Pickles, 2012).

People with ASD display a range of IQ scores. It is estimated that approximately 38% of individuals with ASD have intellectual disabilities (referred to previously as *mental retardation* and defined as an IQ score less than 70, comparable deficits in adaptive functioning, and present before the age of 18; Baio, 2012). IQ measures are used to determine prognosis: The higher children score on IQ tests, the less likely they are to need extensive support by family members or people in the helping professions. Conversely, young children with ASD who score lower on IQ tests are more likely to be severely delayed in acquiring communication skills and to need a great deal of educational and social support as they grow older.

Kanner (1971) followed up on the original 11 children he identified with "autistic disturbances of affective contact" 28 years after he first had contact with them. He determined that only two of the adults were "success stories" and an additional one achieved a "state of limited but positive usefulness" (p. 143). Two thirds of the remaining adults were living in institutions. Unfortunately, there is a dearth of long-term prospective studies on the course of ASD (Howlin, 2005; Rutter, 2011a).

Some have argued that the outcome studies that exist may need to be reconceptualized. For example, Henninger and Taylor (2013) suggested that it may be valuable to consider the person–environment fit when assessing the quality of outcomes. In other words, if living arrangements, employment opportunities, and available peers for socializing are available in ways that are adapted to the needs of the person with ASD, the outcomes may be more positive than if they are not. This is not a function of ASD per se but of whether and how supports are provided to assist with success in adulthood. How people with ASD fare in later life is therefore a product of their behaviors and how environments are adapted to fit their needs. This is an important point to raise for parents who are concerned about how their child will do as an adult; it is helpful to know that there is room to affect the outcomes. (For an important example of one family's successful efforts, see Turnbull & Turnbull, 2011.)

EPIDEMIOLOGY OF ASD

Current estimates of the rates of ASD are based on the previous *DSM–IV–TR* and *ICD–10* criteria (Lord & Bishop, 2010). ASD was once thought to be a rare disorder (e.g., one in 10,000 births), although more recent estimates of its occurrence show an increase in its prevalence. Baio

---

Clinical Concerns: Genetic Counseling

One of the more pressing questions asked by parents who already have one child with ASD is whether a second child might be born with the condition. Previously, the likelihood of a second sibling also being diagnosed with ASD was estimated at between 4% and 10%—higher than the 1% in the general population but certainly a relatively low risk. However, more recent work suggests that the probability of a younger sibling receiving the diagnosis when an older sibling has ASD may be almost 19% (Ozonoff et al., 2011). Because assessment of the siblings ended at around 36 months, milder forms of ASD (e.g., Asperger's type) may not have been identified, which means that the prevalence rate might be even higher. This increase may be due in part to the general increase in the diagnosis of ASD described previously, although studies routinely show many siblings demonstrating some impairments in social-cognitive skills even if not receiving a formal diagnosis of ASD (Silverman et al., 2002). Obviously this information is important to parents wishing to make informed decisions about the size of their family.

(2012) reported that in 2008, one in every 88 children in the United States had been labeled with some form of ASD, with one in 54 boys and one in 252 girls having the diagnosis. Most of the increase in incidence rates may be the result of changes in diagnostic criteria over the years (Miller et al., 2013) as well as increased awareness on the part of professionals and the general public (Fombonne, Quirke, & Hagen, 2011). However, the reasons behind these changes are complex; interested readers can find several thoughtful papers on the topic (e.g., Fombonne et al., 2011; Liu & Bearman, 2012).

There is additional concern that diagnostic inconsistencies across clinicians may contribute to this rise (e.g., Lord, Petkova, et al., 2012). In other words, more individuals are being labeled with various autism-related disorders because the *DSM–IV–TR* criteria were being applied more broadly. One of the reasons may be due to certain pressures to apply the diagnosis more widely. Some parents, for example, encourage a diagnosis in their children because often schools provide more extensive services for students with a diagnosis of ASD as opposed to other related diagnoses (e.g., learning disorder, intellectual disability; Elsabbagh, Divan, et al., 2012). However, other environmental factors (e.g., prenatal exposure to toxic chemicals) cannot yet be ruled out as contributing to some increase in the numbers of persons with this disorder. The rates of ASD worldwide vary, but it is present in every country studied (Elsabbagh, Divan, et al., 2012; Kim et al., 2011).

Gender differences are apparent in ASD, with the average reported male:female ratio being 4.4:1 (Fombonne et al., 2011). Most people with ASD develop the associated symptoms before the age of 36 months (American Psychiatric Association, 2000).

Research from the London School of Economics and the University of Pennsylvania calculated that the annual costs associated with providing care for these persons is a stunning $126 billion in the United States alone (Knapp, 2012). The cost to care for a person with ASD over a lifetime is estimated to be between $1.4 million and $3.2 million in the United States, with comparable costs (£900,00 and £1.5 million) reported in the United Kingdom (M. L. Ganz, 2007; Knapp, Romeo, & Beecham, 2009).

SUMMARY

ASD is a neurodevelopmental disorder whose core deficits involve disruption of social communication and social interaction. In addition, those with ASD display restricted interests and repetitive behaviors. *DSM–5* combines previously distinct disorders (i.e., Asperger's disorder, autistic disorder, childhood disintegrative disorder, and pervasive developmental disorder not otherwise specified) into one umbrella disorder: autism spectrum disorder. The spectrum is represented by levels of severity for the separate social communication and restricted and repetitive behaviors. It is also generally recognized that the course of this disorder differs across individuals during early childhood and that outcomes can vary widely.

3

Etiology

Research on the etiology of autism spectrum disorder (ASD) spans the range of multidimensional influences (e.g., genetics; neuroscience; behavioral and cognitive influences; emotional, cultural, social, and interpersonal factors; life-span development). In fact, the array of information about the origins and development of this spectrum of disorders is among the most complex of any of the psychological and psychiatric disorders (Durand, 2011b; Durand & Barlow, 2010). This picture is further complicated by the wide range of manifestations of individuals affected by ASD. Because of the vast literature in this area, a comprehensive review is beyond the scope of this guide. The goal of this chapter, therefore, is to present the more reliable and accepted findings, with a particular emphasis on those influences that are important for clinical decision-making.

It is generally agreed that ASD does not have a single cause and that there are several (or many) "autisms" (Durand, 2011b; Volkmar, Klin, Schultz, & State, 2009). A number of biological contributions may combine with

http://dx.doi.org/10.1037/14283-002
Autism Spectrum Disorder: A Clinical Guide for General Practitioners, by V. M. Durand

environmental influences to result in the unusual behaviors of people with ASD. The great majority of the research on the etiology of ASD has been and continues to be conducted on persons with the classic Kanner's autism; much less information is available on Asperger's type ASD (Klin, 2011).

The historical context of theories about the cause of ASD played an important role in early treatments and also in how professionals first viewed the role of parents (especially mothers) in this disorder. The chapter describes the historical context, the central role of genetics, and an overview of research on gene × environment interactions and the effects of those interactions on the developing brain in ASD. The chapter ends with a description of some recent work about how these changes in the brain may be affecting the social communicative skills and other behaviors of persons with ASD and how these changes may influence how others interact with them (i.e., reciprocal gene–environment influences). The clinical implications of each of these areas of research are delineated.

HISTORICAL VIEWS

Early theorists viewed the classic Kanner's autism as the result of failed parenting (Bettelheim, 1967; Ferster, 1961; Tinbergen & Tinbergen, 1972). Mothers and fathers of children with autism were characterized as perfectionistic, cold, and aloof (Kanner, 1949), with relatively high socioeconomic status (J. Allen, DeMyer, Norton, Pontius, & Yang, 1971; Cox, Rutter, Newman, & Bartak, 1975) and higher IQs than the general population (Kanner, 1943). Descriptions such as these inspired theories that held parents responsible for their children's unusual behaviors. These views were devastating to a generation of parents, who felt guilty and responsible for their children's problems.

In a telling and important study, Lorna Wing (1980) surveyed an entire area of southeast London for children with "classic autism" and those with intellectual disability but without ASD. When she looked at the socioeconomic status of the fathers of these children and the general social class of other fathers in that region (as defined by their occupation), she observed no differences in the groups. However, she did note that fathers of children with ASD of higher social class were more likely to be members of the National Society of Autistic Children. This was an important observation because previous studies of families of these children recruited samples from these types of organizations. Therefore, the early observations of differences in families may have resulted from selection bias, meaning that they inadvertently studied families with higher socioeconomic status than the general population of parents of children with ASD. More sophisticated research using larger and broader samples of children and families suggests that the parents of individuals with the classic form of autism may not differ substantially in socioeconomic status from parents of typically developing children (Bhasin & Schendel, 2007). Other research on family members suggests that they may differ from the general population on certain personality characteristics (e.g., aloofness, rigidity; e.g., Seidman, Yirmiya, Milshtein, Ebstein, & Levi, 2012). In any case, we now know that how these mothers and fathers parented their children did not lead to the social communication problems or the restricted and repetitive patterns of behaviors.

Other theories about the origins of ASD were based on the unusual speech patterns of some individuals, namely, their tendency to avoid first-person pronouns such as *I* and *me* and to use *he* and *she* instead. For example, if you ask a child with ASD, "Do you want something to drink?" he might say, "He wants something to drink" (meaning "I want something to drink"). This observation led some to theorize whether ASD involves a lack of self-awareness (Goldfarb, 1963; Mahler, 1952). Theorists suggested that the withdrawal seen among people with ASD reflected a lack of awareness of their own existence. However, later research (e.g., Lind & Bowler, 2009) demonstrated that some people with this disorder do exhibit self-awareness that follows a developmental progression. Just like children without ASD, those with cognitive abilities below the level expected for a child of 18 to 24 months show little or no self-recognition, but those with more advanced abilities do demonstrate self-awareness. Self-concept may be lacking when people with ASD also have cognitive disabilities or delays, but a lack of self-concept is not characteristic of the disorder itself.

The phenomenon of echolalia, repeating a word or phrase spoken by another person, was once believed to be a defining albeit unusual characteristic of this disorder. Subsequent work in developmental psychopathology, however, demonstrated that repeating the speech of others is part of the normally developing language skills observed in most young children (Bartak & Rutter, 1974; M. Dawson, Mottron, & Gernsbacher, 2008). Even a behavior as disturbing as the self-injurious behavior sometimes seen in people with ASD (e.g., head banging) is observed in milder forms among typically developing infants (De Lissovoy, 1962). This type of research has helped clinicians isolate the facts from the myths about ASD and clarify the role of development in the disorder.

Early views of ASD considered that the unusual behaviors of these individuals were more consistent with developmental delays in communication and social skills on par with individuals with intellectual disabilities. For example, Lovaas and Smith (1989) proposed that

> (a) autistic children's behaviors are consistent with laws of learning derived from the behavior of other organisms; (b) autistic children have many separate behavioral difficulties best described as a developmental delay; (c) despite their difficulties, many autistic children learn as much as other human beings in certain environments; and (d) their difficulties can be viewed as a mismatch between a deviant nervous system and average or typical environments rather than as a disease. (p. 17)

In other words, much of the problem in ASD was a function of learning problems, and, theoretically, children with ASD could all be taught using basic learning principles.

At present, few workers in the field of ASD believe that psychological or social influences play a major role in the development of this disorder. To the relief of many families, it is now clear that parenting style is not responsible for ASD. In addition, it is also clear that ASD differs fundamentally from simple developmental delay and involves a complex series of developmental changes that stem from neurological difficulties in the social brain. These changes influence not only what the developing child learns but also how the child learns. Deficits in such skills as socialization and communication and restricted and repetitive behaviors appear to have biological origins, although environmental interventions can be successful in mitigating the severity of these difficulties.

GENETIC INFLUENCES

It is now abundantly clear that ASD has a genetic component, with the best evidence suggesting moderate genetic heritability (Hallmayer et al., 2011; Rutter, 2011a). What is also evident is that the genetics of ASD is highly complex (Addington & Rapoport, 2012; Caglayan, 2010; Klei et al., 2012). I often use a metaphor as an aid for describing to families this complexity: Studying the genes that cause ASD is akin to investigating how arriving passengers at JFK airport in New York traveled there. Although all landed in the same place, the number of permutations and combinations of flights from other airports and connecting flights both domestically and internationally is staggering. Unfortunately, the genetics of ASD is equally complex, a fact that complicates the understanding of this spectrum of disorders and the identification of possible interventions. Numerous genes on a number of chromosomes have already been implicated in some way in the presentation of ASD (Li, Zou, & Brown, 2012). As with other psychological disorders (e.g., schizophrenia), in most cases of ASD many genes are involved but each one has only a relatively small effect (Durand & Barlow, 2010).

Genes are sections of DNA found on chromosomes and are responsible for making proteins that build, regulate, and maintain the systems of our bodies. In their simplest form we tend to think of genetic "problems" in terms of having genes turned off (i.e., not making proteins) when they should be turned on and vice versa. However, in the case of ASD, research is finding that in many cases mutations occur that either create extra copies of a gene on one chromosome or result in the deletion of genes (called *copy number variants;* Luo et al., 2012). Because our DNA is structured to function with corresponding or matching pairs of genes on each chromosome, the additions or deletions of one or more genes result in disrupted development. What is also being discovered is that these types of mutations can be present in a child even if the mother or father does not have these copy number variants. Mutations in genes can occur initially in one family member as a result of a mutation in a germ cell (egg or sperm) of one of the parents or in the fertilized egg after conception (called *de novo mutations*), and there is growing evidence that some persons with ASD display these types of mutations (Kong et al., 2012; Sanders et al., 2012; Sebat et al., 2007). It is not clear why these changes in genetic material occur, but they may increase risk of ASD by 5 to 20 times (Neale et al., 2012). These de novo mutations help explain why this disorder can occur in families who do not have a familial history of ASD.

Clinical Concerns: Parental Guilt

In the late 1960s and 1970s, many believed that mothers of children with ASD caused their children to have these disorders. Failed parenting—not being affectionate enough in early childhood (*refrigerator mothers*)—was thought to result in the social difficulties experienced by these children (Bettelheim, 1967). Such views led many mothers to feel overwhelming guilt that they had somehow caused their own children to turn away from them and from others. And now, even though clinicians discount parenting style as a major cause of ASD, the evidence for the role of genetics sometimes leads parents to experience "genetic guilt," or a sense of responsibility for the child's disorder because of passed-on genetic material. Although in some cases there is a genetic component, it is also true that other cases are caused by changes in genes prior to conception or in utero. In families without any similar cases of ASD or related disorders, these mutations may be at least partially responsible (Geschwind, 2009). Clinicians may be able to assist parents who feel guilty about their child's ASD by educating them about how complicated the disorder is and how unpredictable birth outcomes can be for individual children and families. Currently, there are no simple genetic tests that can predict definitively whether children will or will not have ASD.

Syndromic and Nonsyndromic ASD

Research on the genetics of ASD reveals a variety of syndromes that are associated with the symptoms of the disorder (referred to as *syndromic autism*) as well as specific gene changes that result in these symptoms (referred to as *nonsyndromic autism;* Caglayan, 2010). Approximately 10% of those diagnosed with ASD would fall into the syndromic category (Persico & Bourgeron, 2006). Rett's syndrome, for example, was previously included under the broad category of "pervasive developmental disorders" (which included autistic disorder and Asperger's disorder) because the children with this syndrome displayed the social communication and behavioral deficits characteristic of ASD. The decision (reflected in the fifth edition of the *Diagnostic and Statistical Manual of Mental Disorders [DSM–5];* American Psychiatric Association, 2013) to remove this syndrome as part of the general label of autism spectrum disorder occurred because (a) individuals displayed the behaviors associated with ASD for a short period of time and (b) it may be more valuable to use the clinical specifier "Associated with Known Medical Disorder or Genetic Condition" to make clear that the behaviors had a clearly identifiable origin (American Psychiatric Association, 2013).

More common among these syndromes are fragile X (a condition caused by changes in part of the X chromosome), Angelman syndrome (caused by a duplication of a gene on chromosome 15 and characterized by a lack of speech, seizures, and walking and balance disorders), and Smith-Lemi-Opitz (caused by a defect in cholesterol synthesis). Many of these syndromes are associated with intellectual disability, which can sometimes complicate distinguishing ASD separately from the intellectual disability (Dykens & Lense, 2011). In other words, ongoing problems with social communication and challenging behavior are frequent in persons with intellectual disability as a function of their cognitive delays and may not suggest the presence of ASD. Also, the prevalence of ASD among persons with some of these syndromes is at a rate that is similar to that in the general population, which may call into question the association of these syndromes with ASD.

Nonsyndromic autism is believed to characterize about 90% of the cases of ASD (Persico & Bourgeron, 2006). Several genes that appear to result in ASD are found on the X chromosome (e.g., mutations found at the following locations: Xq13.1, Xp22.33, Xq28). Because males have only one X chromosome, any mutations on that chromosome will be expressed and will influence later development. This may explain the much higher prevalence of ASD among males than females (one in 54 boys vs. one in 252 girls; Baio, 2012).

One area that is receiving attention involves the genes responsible for the brain chemical oxytocin. Because oxytocin is shown to have a role in how we bond with others and in our social memory, researchers are looking at whether genes responsible for this neurochemical (oxytocin receptor genes) are involved with the disorder. Preliminary work has identified an association between ASD and an oxytocin receptor gene (Wermter, et al., 2010). However, when diverse samples are studied (including the range of persons with ASD), this association disappears (Tansey et al., 2010), which suggests that certain subpopulations with ASD may be discovered based on these genetic profiles. From a clinical perspective, some applied research shows modest improvements in repetitive behaviors and social cognition among some with ASD when given oxytocin (e.g., Domes, Heinrichs, Michel, Berger, & Herpertz, 2007; Guastella et al., 2010; Hollander et al., 2003).

Understanding the genetic bases of ASD is a critical research goal. However, it is important to emphasize that knowing that a person has a gene or genes for a particular disorder leads to probabilistic information only. In other words, the presence of a gene for a disorder is not deterministic; it does not mean that the disease or disorder will manifest itself. (One exception is Huntington's disease, which is caused by a genetic defect on Chromosome 4; anyone who has this gene [*huntingtin*] will ultimately develop the disease [Ross & Tabrizi, 2011]. However, deterministic genes such as the Huntington's gene are rare.) More common are genes that make small contributions (with other genes) to create the ultimate outcome (Fraser & Marcotte, 2004). These genes are referred to as *probabilistic*, and researchers are identifying dozens of genes that in certain combinations lead to the symptoms of ASD. So even if researchers identify the full range of genes involved in ASD and can identify them in individuals, predicting what will happen in one particular individual will remain probabilistic; the outcomes and course of the disorder cannot be predicted with certainty.

Clinical Concerns: Controversies Over Genetic Testing

Despite rapid advances in our understanding of the complexities of the genetics of ASD, the field has not yet sufficiently progressed for this information to be used to provide precise genetic counseling (Jordan & Tsai, 2010). For instance, although there are most certainly genetic influences on ASD, recent work points to an important role for de novo mutations (genetic changes that were not present in either parent; e.g., Sebat et al., 2007), thus making predictions more complex. Additionally, no definitive biological markers for ASD exist that allow for prenatal identification. As a result, clinicians need to be cautious when providing advice to families. (For professional guidelines for genetic testing, see Committee on Bioethics, Committee on Genetics, and The American College of Medical Genetics and Genomics Social Ethical and Legal Issues Committee, 2013.)

Some have argued that children who have been diagnosed with ASD should undergo genetic testing (Herman et al., 2007; Lintas & Persico, 2009; Shen et al., 2010). The technology for identifying even extremely rare genetic mutations improves constantly. But should families go through the expense of genetic testing for their child with ASD, which can cost several thousand dollars? Currently, the information that can be obtained through such testing can identify genetic mutations. However, this knowledge does not convey information about the course of the disorder, nor does it contribute to treatment recommendations. Although it may provide some parents with at least partial answers about the possible origins of their child's ASD (e.g., a deletion on a particular chromosome), there are no genetic treatments for these mutations and knowing this does not direct clinicians with their efforts to provide effective intervention.

Perhaps even more controversial are the recommendations to conduct prenatal genetic testing (e.g., Wapner, 2012). The same types of genetic testing that can be conducted on a child can also be carried out on a developing fetus. These tests can give parents information early on in the pregnancy if there are genetic conditions present in utero. However, because ASD is caused by multiple influences, these types of tests cannot provide definitive information about the probability of the child's developing ASD or its eventual severity. Moreover, the same ethical issues would arise, for example, in the case of genetic screening for Down syndrome. Unlike genetic testing for ASD, knowing soon after conception that the developing fetus has an extra 21st chromosome (i.e., Down syndrome) does predict that the child will have the disorder. Importantly, however, information about this chromosomal abnormality does not convey information about the eventual severity of the disorder. Will the child have mild or more severe intellectual disabilities? Will the physical problems associated with the disorder (e.g., cardiac problems) be present, and will they be life threatening? Despite this lack of information, some estimate that a prenatal diagnosis of Down syndrome leads to a choice for an elective abortion about 25% of the time (Bishop, Huether, Torfs, Lorey, & Deddens, 1997). Prenatal testing for Down syndrome cannot assist parents with information about the outcomes, and this is even more relevant in the case of ASD. Knowing that a fetus has a specific mutation that is associated with ASD tells very little about how that child will develop after birth.

Gene × Environment Interactions

ASD represents a variation in neurodevelopment. In other words, atypical changes take place in the developing brain over time. Some of these changes are attributed to the genetic differences just described (e.g., de novo copy number variants, rare mutations). However, it is now clear that an important area of study in efforts to understand the development of ASD is how environmental influences can interact with these genetic influences (Szatmari, 2011). In the case of ASD, the environmental factors being explored are diverse. This section describes briefly some areas of ongoing research.

It is known that exposure to toxins such as pesticides, valproate, or maternal rubella during pregnancy can interact with genetic material to cause harmful changes in their functioning. Research on ASD is looking at the role of insecticides, for example, on creating damage through a process called *oxidative stress* (a disruption in the normal process by which cells rid themselves of harmful free radicals [Chauhan & Chauhan, 2006]). Some work suggests that certain occurrences of the genetic mutations observed in groups of persons with ASD make them particularly susceptible to the damaging effects of these types of toxins (Shelton, Hertz-Picciotto, & Pessah, 2012). This gene × environment interaction illustrates how complex the study of the causes of ASD can be for researchers.

Other prenatal events are also possibly linked to ASD. For example, several studies suggest that prolonged episodes of maternal fever appear to increase the risk of ASD in the newborn (e.g., Atladóttir, Henriksen, Schendel, & Parner, 2012). On the other hand, there are mixed results when researchers study the possible influence of maternal influenza infection during pregnancy (Atladóttir et al., 2012; Zerbo et al., 2013). Research has also targeted the role of metabolic conditions during pregnancy, such as diabetes, hypertension, and obesity in the development of ASD. In one of the largest investigations of its kind, the CHARGE (Childhood Autism Risks from Genetics and the Environment) study, a population-based, case-control investigation, looked at 517 children with ASD, 172 developmental delays but no ASD, and 315 controls, all between the ages of 2 and 5 years. In one analysis of the data, researchers found increased risk for ASD when mothers had one or more of these metabolic conditions during pregnancy (Krakowiak et al., 2012). All in all, it appears that prenatal exposure to a range of conditions that compromise a pregnancy may increase the risk of ASD, with no one factor predominating (Gardener, Spiegelman, & Buka, 2011; Volk, Lurmann, Penfold, Hertz-Picciotto, & McConnell, 2013).

The implications for clinicians who may work with family members focus on education and recommendations for planning for future pregnancies. First, it is obvious that not all mothers who are exposed to toxins, high fevers, or influenza viruses or who have a range of metabolic conditions during pregnancy ultimately give birth to children with ASD.

Although these factors may increase risk, the genetic influences described previously also come into play. At the same time, if parents have a child with ASD and anticipate having more children, the risk may be reduced with good prenatal care (e.g., the use of prenatal vitamins and supplements, maternal vaccinations for the flu).

The risk of having a child with ASD appears to increase in older parents. One group of researchers in Israel, for example, found that fathers 40 years old and older were more than 5 times more likely to have a child with ASD than were fathers under the age of 30 (Reichenberg et al., 2006). The same correlation does seem to hold up for maternal age (Croen, Najjar, Fireman, & Grether, 2007; Durkin et al., 2008; Parner et al., 2012). How this association occurs is not fully understood, but it is tempting to suggest that the role of de novo mutations is at least partly to blame. In other words, as the sperm and eggs age, they are more likely to be exposed to various toxins that can increase the risk of these types of genetic changes. Again, the clinical implications are clear. Parents who are older (i.e., above age 40) who already have a child with ASD may be at greater risk for having another child with the disorder. Providing clients in this situation with such information can assist them with their decision making.

Clinical Concerns: The Role of Vaccines in ASD

One of the most controversial questions within the field of ASD over the past 2 decades has been the possible role of the measles, mumps, and rubella (MMR) vaccine, the preservative used in some vaccines (thimerosal, a mercury-based compound that is an antiseptic and antifungal agent), or the general increase in the number of vaccines given to children as causing the increased rates of children diagnosed with ASD (Plotkin, Gerber, & Offit, 2009). The controversy originated with the publication of a paper pointing out that certain children were reported to have been typically developing but then regressed shortly after they received the MMR vaccine. This study had a number of methodological flaws and was later discredited and retracted (Wakefield et al., 1998). Research looking into the connection has consistently found no association. For example, a population study in Yokohama, Japan (where they reduced and eventually stopped administering the MMR vaccine) still found increasing rates of ASD (Honda, Shimizu, & Rutter, 2005). A related theory is that mercury (thimerosal) found in the preservative used in vaccines interacted with neurodevelopment in young children to cause the symptoms of ASD. In addition, because the number of different vaccines increased from the 1980s (simultaneously with the rise in diagnosis of ASD), some researchers speculated that this somehow overwhelmed or weakened the immune systems of these children (Plotkin et al., 2009) and was responsible for the increases seen in ASD over the past decade. Numerous large epidemiological studies have shown no association between ASD and either thimerosal or increased use of vaccines (Hviid, Stellfeld, Wohlfahrt, & Melbye, 2003; Rutter, 2011a; Stehr-Green, Tull, Stellfeld, Mortenson, & Simpson, 2003). Despite this and other convincing evidence, the correlation between when a child is vaccinated for MMR (12–15 months) and evidence of symptoms of ASD (before 3 years) continues to fuel the belief by many families that there must be some connection. This fear has resulted in significant reductions in vaccinations among all children in the United Kingdom and in the United States (McDonald, Pace, Blue, & Schwartz, 2012). Many families who have a child with ASD delay or skip vaccines for their other children because of this concern (Kuwaik et al., 2012). This is a potential public health concern that can put their children and others at risk for contracting formerly rare diseases.

NEUROLOGICAL INFLUENCES

Research on the nature of brain dysfunction in ASD is advancing at a rapid pace (Minshew, Scherf, Behrmann, & Humphreys, 2011). For example, a great deal of research focuses on deficits in executive functioning (i.e., the ability to organize and control cognitive abilities) in persons with ASD (Yoder & Belmonte, 2011). The latest thinking in this area is that ASD is a developmental neurobiological disorder, meaning that a variety of developmental changes occur in the brains of people with this disorder (Minshew & Keller, 2010). In the typically developing brain, a series of developmental changes occur, including the creation and movement of neurons, the creation of dendritic arbors (branches of the neurons involved with communicating with other neurons) and synaptic connections, and eventually dendritic pruning and programmed cell death. This latter process essentially makes the brain more efficient by getting rid of unused or duplicative brain cells. Unfortunately, changes at any one of these stages can result in major disruptions later in the process. These changes, although not yet fully understood, may account for both the social communication and behavioral difficulties as well as the strengths displayed by those with ASD.

Leo Kanner noted in a follow-up of his original 11 individuals with autism that four of these children had unusually large heads (Kanner, 1971). Although not considered a characteristic of the disorder, contemporary research has revisited this observation. One of the better understood changes that appears common in the developing brains of persons with ASD is an early (age 6 months) increase in white matter development followed by a plateau effect through later toddlerhood (age 12 months; Wolff et al., 2012). White matter in the brain (as opposed to gray matter) is thought to serve as a relay pathway for different parts of the brain and to coordinate brain activity. In this case excessive brain cell development may not be a good thing; it may result in abnormal development of the social brain (Courchesne, Webb, & Schumann, 2011).

One of the more reliable findings of brain involvement in ASD is a decrease in the number of Purkinje cells, which results in the reduction of the size of cerebellum (G. Allen & Courchesne, 2003; S. H. Fatemi et al., 2002). These cells are primarily involved in motor responses, and the pattern of their loss in those with ASD suggests that they are damaged prenatally (S. Fatemi et al., 2012). The role of Purkinje cells in ASD is not yet clear and, as seen before, may represent a promising area to search for subgroups of persons with ASD, especially those who may have comorbid motor symptom difficulties (e.g., fine motor problems).

One intriguing area of study involves research on the amygdala, the area of the brain that is involved in emotions such as anxiety and fear. Researchers who studied the brains of people with ASD after they died noted that adults with and without the disorder have amygdalae of about the same size but that those with ASD have fewer neurons in this structure (Schumann & Amaral, 2006). Earlier research showed that young children with ASD actually have a larger amygdala. One theory is that the amygdala in children with ASD is enlarged early in life, influencing their levels of anxiety and fear (perhaps contributing to their social withdrawal). With continued stress, the release of the stress hormone cortisol damages the amygdala, causing the relative absence of these neurons in adulthood. The damaged amygdala may account for the different ways in which people with ASD respond to social situations (Lombardo, Chakrabarti, & Baron-Cohen, 2009). Some research on obsessive–compulsive disorder suggests the role of abnormal activity in the amygdala in the origins of this disorder (e.g., van den Heuvel et al., 2004). The similarities between the compulsive behaviors of persons with obsessive–compulsive disorder (e.g., rituals that help reduce the anxiety associated with obsessive thoughts) resemble some of the repetitive behaviors exhibited by those with ASD (e.g., Maria's lining up toys and silverware and becoming upset if they were disturbed) and may help explain their causes.

Facial Recognition and Processing

People with ASD have difficulty interacting with others and often prefer "things" to people. Recent research on children with ASD and with infants without these disorders may shed some light on this characteristic problem and how it might develop. For example, some research has shown that individuals with ASD tend to avoid looking at pictures of faces (G. Dawson, Carver, et al., 2002; Remington, Campbell, & Swettenham, 2012). One study looked at infants at risk for ASD (i.e., those with a family member having ASD) and those not at risk and measured their brain activity when exposed to pictures of faces (Elsabbagh, Mercure, et al., 2012). Researchers then followed the children to see who was later diagnosed with ASD at 36 months and found that those with ASD had different brain responses to faces at 6 to 10 months than those without ASD. In other words, even before it was clear that infants had ASD, their social brains were reacting differently (Elsabbagh et al., 2009).

Obviously, if you are avoiding looking at people, you will be at a major disadvantage when trying to learn communication and social skills. In an important study with typically developing infants, researchers found that infants age 4 months look at a speaker's face (Lewkowicz & Hansen-Tift, 2012). Then, between 4 and 8 months of age they switch their attention from the eyes of the speaker to the mouth to pick up audiovisual cues. They then begin a shift back to the eyes at 12 months. What this means is that infants are not just listening to speech but are also learning by watching the eyes and mouth of the speaker. Therefore, if infants with ASD are not watching faces they will be at a distinct disadvantage. But why would they avoid looking at faces?

Some have theorized that those with ASD experience anxiety when they come into contact with people, and so they avoid them. But when researchers have looked at arousal, they often get mixed results. In one study, people with and without ASD looked at pictures of faces at two different times (Kleinhans et al., 2009). Researchers monitored their brain activity through functional magnetic resonance imaging and found that the first time they showed the picture of a face, both groups had increased arousal in the amygdala (a part of the brain previously seen as potentially involved with ASD). A new, unfamiliar face may be mildly anxiety producing for anyone because of all the new features to consider. When the picture was displayed a second time, participants in the control group habituated, meaning that they did not have the same hyperarousal response. However, the people with ASD did not habituate and continued to show hyperarousal. Without getting used to faces, people with ASD may experience stimulus overload each time they see a person. This study and others (e.g., Kliemann, Dziobek, Hatri, Baudewig, & Heekeren, 2012; Swartz, Wiggins, Carrasco, Lord, & Monk, 2013) may help to (a) make sense of why people with ASD avoid faces and (b) map the developmental progression of the problems later seen in persons with ASD, including their social impairments and communication difficulties. This type of research may help explain why individuals with ASD lack or are impaired in joint attention (G. Dawson, Munson, et al., 2002).

Going back to the case of Maria, one observation of her in a preschool classroom may help integrate these observations about facial processing and the learning difficulties of children with ASD. She was seated at a table and her teacher was trying to get her to point to a picture she labeled ("Maria, point to the picture of the dog"). Maria was squirming in her chair and looking around the room, not focusing on any particular person or thing. After a few minutes, with Maria still not pointing to the picture without the teacher physically taking her hand to point to it, the teacher handed her an iPad; she was rewarding Maria for sitting without getting out of her seat for 5 minutes. Maria quickly plugged in her headphones into the tablet, turned it on, tapped the video icon, selected a movie, fast forwarded it to a particular place, and watched the movie intently. Her teacher noted, "She's better at using that than I am." The previously described research suggests that her difficulties responding to adult-presented requests might have had more to do with facial aversion (and perhaps generalized aversion to others) than an inability to understand complex tasks. This basic research might be used to help children like Maria learn through technology and also to help them reduce their fear reaction to human faces. I explore these issues further in Chapter 6.

Theory of Mind

One social process that is being researched extensively is the inability of persons with ASD to interpret their own intentions and emotions and those of others. This ability to attribute subjective mental states (referred to as *theory of mind*) appears to be extremely important for learning important social skills (Baron-Cohen, 1997; Baron-Cohen, Tager-Flusberg, & Cohen, 2000). For example, if a woman walks toward you in a slow manner with her head down, you immediately notice these nonverbal signals and attempt to determine what she might be thinking or feeling (e.g., "She looks so sad. I wonder what happened to her?"). No one teaches us as children to do this. Instead, our natural ability to empathize or "feel" the emotions of others and our inherent interest in people seem to combine to develop the tendency to interpret the intentions of others.

However, if this interest in the thoughts and feelings of others is impaired or absent, successful social exchanges become much more difficult. For example, Jacob (see Chapter 1) once described how he tried to talk with a young woman at a coffee shop. He saw her talking with a group of other young women, and he walked over to her because he thought she was pretty. He introduced himself and she looked at him, smiled slightly and said "Hi," but then turned around to go back to her conversation. Jacob did not understand that even though she said hello to him, her turning away was a signal that she was not interested in a conversation with him. His response was to walk to the other side of the group so he was facing her and started asking her if she was interested in *Star Wars*. When she asked him to leave them alone, he was confused. He interpreted her saying hello back as a sign she liked him, and he did not read the nonverbal signals as just the opposite.

Some research suggests that individuals with Asperger's type ASD seem to do better at theory of mind tasks as they enter adolescence. Some adolescents with ASD seem to be able to pick out instances of complex social interactions such as the use of sarcasm or to be able to infer mental states in others when presented with social stories (i.e., narratives of social exchanges; Scheeren, de Rosnay, Koot, & Begeer, 2013). It should be pointed out, however, that this may represent a rote learned ability to interpret these situations. It may not represent an improvement in the underlying ability to feel the emotions of others (empathy), the absence of which will continue to interfere with socialization. Jacob, for example, was beginning to learn that when young women he approached looked away from him after he started talking, that meant they were not interested in him. However, he could not pick up more subtle social cues, such as looking away and not smiling, as signs of disinterest. Efforts to teach theory of mind skills to persons with ASD suggest that although many can learn to report back a logical understanding of the intent of verbal and nonverbal cues, effects on empathy and overall improvements in social skills are not usually reported (e.g., Begeer et al., 2011). Teaching these skills in the absence of their "feeling" what others feel complicates learning appropriate social skills.

Reciprocal Gene–Environment Model

The reciprocal gene–environment model suggests that people with a genetic predisposition for a disorder may also have a genetic tendency to create environmental risk factors that promote the disorder. In the case of young children with ASD, their social aversion and unusual behaviors can cause others to treat them differently from typically developing children. This, in turn, may further exacerbate problems in development as the child grows older. For example, in work with children who have significant behavior problems such as aggression and tantrums, some parents and teachers change the way they handle the child in order to avoid triggering an outburst (Durand, 2011c; Steed & Durand, 2013). A teacher may find that difficult academic tasks increase the risk of an outburst, and they therefore choose not to assign such tasks to children with Asperger's type ASD despite their cognitive ability to complete them. This results in delays in academic progress. Parents, for example, often describe how their child may act out in public; they find themselves not taking their child to parks or the homes of other children for fear of disruption or that other children will see their child as odd. This limits social opportunities to learn from peers and can contribute to an increase in social delays (Chapter 7 outlines how to help these families). It is expected that more research on these types of reciprocal gene–environment influences will aid future intervention efforts for children with ASD (G. Dawson, 2008).

SUMMARY

The genetic and neurobiological research on ASD points to a complex series of developmental events that lead to the social communicative deficits observed in this population. An important early influence may be that these individuals are poised to respond benignly or negatively to others (especially faces). Decreased social attention and decreased social motivation in the first months of life begin to derail typical development of important skills such as social interaction and communication skills (G. Dawson et al., 2012; M. H. Johnson et al., 2005; Mundy & Neal, 2000). Not looking at other faces impedes learning through imitation and affects social development in general. This may also impact the development of the ability to empathize with the thoughts and feelings of others and to learn theory of mind. What remains unclear is how the different presentations of ASD (e.g., Kanner's type, Asperger's type) occur in this population. What is clear, however, is that early intervention is essential in order to help young children with ASD. As will be seen in the treatment chapter, focused and intensive intervention for young children with ASD helps many to make major improvements in cognitive and social abilities, and there is growing evidence that this type of behavioral intervention also may make direct changes in the developing social brain (G. Dawson et al., 2012; Voos et al., 2013). In other words, it may be possible to preempt some of the developmental consequences of early social irregularities by using behavioral intervention techniques to improve social attention and motivation.

4

Comorbid Conditions

Individuals with ASD often have comorbid disorders, which speaks to the need for a comprehensive assessment beyond the presence of the symptoms of the disorder. Although not all of these comorbid disorders are symptomatic of ASD, they can contribute to how one intervenes with each individual. Some of the common conditions may help further our understanding of the different "autisms" and suggest meaningful subgroups. In addition, some of these difficulties are of significant concern to families (e.g., sleep problems, gastrointestinal difficulties) and can contribute to the daily stress these families face.

INTELLECTUAL DISABILITY

Among those with the Kanner's type of ASD, the most common co-occurring problem is intellectual disability (formerly referred to as *mental retardation*), with approximately two thirds scoring significantly

http://dx.doi.org/10.1037/14283-003
Autism Spectrum Disorder: A Clinical Guide for General Practitioners, by V. M. Durand
Copyright © 2014 by the American Psychological Association. All rights reserved.

below average on IQ tests (Dykens & Lense, 2011). In contrast, those with the Asperger's type do not show these cognitive delays, yet they have more qualitative difficulties with language and socialization. Often those with ASD associated with a known genetic syndrome (e.g., fragile X, Angelman syndrome, tuberous sclerosis) are also likely to have mild to profound cognitive impairments. The presence of intellectual disability along with the core symptoms of ASD (social communicative skills deficits and restricted interests and repetitive behaviors) can complicate efforts to provide educational services. Additionally, the presence of intellectual disabilities can be predictive of poorer later outcomes for these individuals (Kanne et al., 2011). Intervention for individuals with ASD and comorbid intellectual disabilities include special education services that focus not only on the symptoms of ASD but also on skills geared toward promoting independence (e.g., washing, eating, dressing; Durand, 2005).

EPILEPSY

A significant portion of individuals with ASD develop seizures as they grow older. One large study of adults who were diagnosed with ASD as children found that 22% of these individuals experienced repeated seizures, which typically developed after the age of 10 (Bolton et al., 2011). Estimates suggest that those with ASD are approximately 10 to 30 times more likely to have epilepsy than the general population; occurrence is increased among those with ASD having intellectual disability (Tuchman, 2011), and the seizures tend to be the more severe whole body events (grand mal or generalized tonic-clonic). Epilepsy was found to be more common among females, those with intellectual disability, and those with poor verbal skills (Bolton et al., 2011). The presence of epilepsy with ASD tends to predict poorer long-term outcomes (Berg & Plioplys, 2012; Tuchman, 2011). Early identification and treatment for seizures may help improve outcomes for these individuals.

ANXIETY DISORDERS

Symptoms of anxiety are commonly reported among persons with ASD (White, Oswald, Ollendick, & Scahill, 2009). It is estimated that roughly 50% to 80% of these individuals can be diagnosed with one or more anxiety disorders, including simple phobias, generalized anxiety disorder, separation anxiety disorder, obsessive–compulsive disorder (OCD), and social phobia (de Bruin, Ferdinand, Meester, de Nijs, & Verheij, 2007; Leyfer et al., 2006; White et al., 2009). One study, for example, found that cortisol (a biological marker for stress and anxiety) levels and reactivity differed among persons with ASD and those without the disorder in situations associated with change or stress (Spratt et al., 2012). More individuals with Asperger's type ASD receive a diagnosis of one or more of these disorders (Szatmari & McConnell, 2011). This may in part be related to difficulty interpreting the behavior of persons with Kanner's type ASD. Maria, for example, would flap her hands excitedly in the presence of noisy groups, which her parents assumed was her attempt to block out or distract herself from noise she disliked. Inappropriate affect is often observed in ASD; a child may smile despite an obvious negative experience (Durand & Mapstone, 1997).

A number of rating scales can be used for more formal assessment of anxiety and related problems in this population (e.g., Social Anxiety Scale for Adolescents [La Greca, 1999]; Multidimensional Anxiety Scale for Children [March, 1999]; Behavioral Assessment System for Children Self-Report of Personality [Reynolds & Kamphaus, 1998]; for a full list of these assessments, see Grondhuis & Aman, 2012, and White et al., 2009). Treatment for these problems with anxiety mirror work with persons not having special needs (cognitive behavior therapy [CBT]; Szatmari & McConnell, 2011). For example, a randomized clinical trial was conducted to evaluate a modified CBT protocol on the anxiety symptoms of 20 children with Asperger's type ASD (Reaven, Blakeley-Smith, Culhane-Shelburne, & Hepburn, 2012). The researchers adapted prior approaches to reduce anxiety in children (e.g., graded exposure, relaxation and deep breathing, strategies for emotion regulation, use of cognitive self-control) for the verbal and cognitive abilities of these children. Approximately 50% of the children who participated in the group treatment program had clinically significant reductions in anxiety. Clinicians with a background in working with youth and who have training in CBT would find the protocol from this work helpful (Reaven, Blakeley-Smith, Nichols, & Hepburn, 2011).

A growing evidence base suggests that modified CBT can be helpful in reducing anxiety symptoms in some individuals with Asperger's type ASD (Chalfant, Rapee, & Carroll, 2007; White et al., 2010; Wood et al., 2009). Although there is little evidence for the effectiveness of antianxiety medications (e.g., SSRIs) in this population (Szatmari & McConnell, 2011), approximately 20% of school-age children with ASD regularly take these medications (Pringle, Colpe, Blumberg, Avila, & Kogan, 2012).

The repetitive behaviors exhibited by some individuals with ASD, and the behavioral outbursts that often accompany attempts to interrupt these behaviors, are thought by some to resemble characteristics of OCD (Jacob, Landeros-Weisenberger, & Leckman, 2011; Taylor & Hollander, 2011). Although the forms of these behaviors often differ between persons with a diagnosis of OCD (e.g., checking, cleaning, counting) and persons with ASD (e.g., lining up objects, touching), the overlap of a motor component and a cognitive component (e.g., perseverative thoughts) suggests a possible connection between the two disorders. Genetic studies suggest that family members of those with ASD are at increased risk for OCD (Jacob et al., 2011). Although there are few treatment studies demonstrating lasting improvements in these behaviors, several studies with small sample sizes suggest some modest improvements in these behaviors using treatments found to be effective with OCD (modifications of exposure and response prevention; Boyd, Woodard, & Bodfish, 2011; Lehmkuhl, Storch, Bodfish, & Geffken, 2008; Reaven & Hepburn, 2003).

MOOD DISORDERS

Reports of depression are common among persons at the more advanced end of the ASD spectrum, with rates approximating 25% to 34% (Ghaziuddin, Ghaziuddin, & Greden, 2002; Mayes, Calhoun, Murray, Ahuja, & Smith, 2011). Often feelings of depression and loneliness are expressed over difficulties creating and maintaining social relationships (Whitehouse, Durkin, Jaquet, & Ziatas, 2009). For example, research suggests that individuals with ASD who possess more insight into their social differences compared with peers report more symptoms of depression (Hedley & Young, 2006). As we saw in the case of Jacob, these reports are more common from parents of those with ASD than self-reports (Butzer & Konstantareas, 2003). Given the communication difficulties observed in individuals with the Kanner's type of ASD, a diagnosis of depression in this group is often made on the basis of parental reports and is therefore somewhat problematic (Mayes, Calhoun, Murray, & Zahid, 2011).

Although there is some indication that teaching social skills may improve self-image and self-reported feelings of depression (e.g., Hedley & Young, 2006), there is not yet a body of work pointing to established treatments in this area. And although the use of pharmacological intervention for depression (SSRIs) is common among typically developing children and youth as well as among those with ASD (Pringle et al., 2012), research documenting these agents' effectiveness in ASD is limited (Szatmari & McConnell, 2011).

ATTENTION-DEFICIT/HYPERACTIVITY DISORDER

The symptoms that are characteristic of attention-deficit/hyperactivity disorder (ADHD)—attention deficit, impulsivity, and hyperactivity—are often observed among individuals with ASD (Mayes & Calhoun, 2007; Mayes, Calhoun, Mayes, & Molitoris, 2012). In addition, behavior problems and neurocognitive deficits are similar in these two groups (Mayes & Calhoun, 2007). Behavioral treatment for the symptoms of ADHD observed in children with ASD parallels that used in classroom and home interventions for children with ADHD (Pfiffner et al., 2011; Volpe, Young, Piana, & Zaslofsky, 2012). Functional behavioral assessments are conducted to assess the functions of behavioral problems, alternative behaviors are encouraged (e.g., teaching a child to request assistance rather than getting out of his or her seat or throwing tantrums), and reinforcement programs are put in place to encourage improved behavior at home and at school. In addition, pharmacological intervention is often used when children with ASD exhibit symptoms of ADHD. It is reported that approximately one third of school-age children with ASD receive stimulant medications for symptoms of ADHD (Pringle et al., 2012), although stimulants seem to be effective for only a minority of individuals with ASD and often have intolerable side effects (Research Units on Pediatric Psychopharmacology Autism Network, 2005).

GASTROINTESTINAL PROBLEMS

The issue of gastrointestinal (GI) problems in ASD took center stage with the publication of the controversial and later retracted study by Wakefield et al. (1998). This study supposedly identified lower GI tract inflammation in 12 children with ASD who regressed after a period of typical development. The authors hypothesized that this regression and co-occurring GI problems were both related to the administration of the measles, mumps, and rubella vaccine. Although this work was later discredited, it did highlight a concern raised by parents for some time: Many of their children had a variety of GI problems, including diarrhea, constipation, and stomach pains (Buie, Campbell, et al., 2010). For example, one large study found that approximately 42% of children with ASD were reported by their parents as having GI problems as compared with 12% of their siblings without ASD (Wang, Tancredi, & Thomas, 2011). Accurate reporting of GI problems can be complicated by communication difficulties, especially among those with Kanner's type ASD (e.g., looking like they are uncomfortable but not being able to say whether and where they hurt). In addition, the eating difficulties can be a contributing cause of GI problems if the child's diet is severely limited (e.g., low in fiber). Stress can serve as a cause of these difficulties. Although individuals with ASD are at risk for symptoms such as constipation and diarrhea, they are not known to be at risk for any specific GI pathologies (Buie, Campbell, et al., 2010). Fortunately, formal medical guidelines for the assessment and treatment of GI symptoms in persons with ASD are available (Buie, Fuchs, et al., 2010).

EATING AND FEEDING PROBLEMS

Children with ASD are often referred to as "picky" or "finicky" when it comes to what they will eat, often avoiding certain tastes or textures of foods or having very limited food preferences (Ledford & Gast, 2006). This refusal can take the form of tantrums if they are prompted to eat specific foods and can escalate to choking, gagging, and vomiting (Schwarz, 2003). Not only is this disturbing to families around mealtimes, but it can also a cause for concern about obtaining proper nutrition and can contribute to GI problems (S. L. Hyman et al., 2012; Sharp et al., 2013). Maria, for example, had a very limited diet and would only eat a certain brand of macaroni and cheese each night for dinner.

Assessment of problems around mealtimes typically includes a behavioral assessment of the child's acceptance and refusal of a range of food types and textures as well as the nature and severity of disruption surrounding food refusal (e.g., Ahearn, Castine, Nault, & Green, 2001). The child is systematically offered bites of different foods, and the number of bites and refusal is recorded. Research on the treatment for food selectivity and refusal is limited mostly to studies with small sample sizes that use some variation of allowing access to preferred foods for increasing acceptance of nonpreferred foods (Matson & Fodstad, 2009). Because of the risk of choking, it is recommended that only clinicians who have experience with feeding difficulties attempt an intervention.

SLEEP DISORDERS

Problems surrounding sleep are common among children with ASD, reportedly affecting 50% to 80% (Couturier et al., 2005; Krakowiak, Goolin-Jones, Hertz-Picciotto, Croen, & Hansen, 2008; Richdale & Schreck, 2009). Children with ASD develop more sleep problems as they move into adolescence, and they tend to continue to experience sleep problems over time (e.g., Goldman, Richdale, Clemons, & Malow, 2012; Sivertsen, Posserud, Gillberg, Lundervold, & Hysing, 2012). The disruption of sleep in this population raises many concerns (Durand, 2013). Experiencing inadequate amounts of sleep affects several systems in the body that can increase the risk of cardiovascular and metabolic disease (Barclay & Gregory, 2013). In addition, poor sleep affects academic and behavioral performance in school (Staples & Bates, 2011) as well as overall emotional states (Berger, Miller, Seifer, Cares, & Lebourgeois, 2012). These effects can be extremely disruptive to other family members, significantly interfering with their own sleep and contributing to their levels of stress.

The main problems reported include insomnia with prolonged sleep latency (i.e., time to fall asleep), disruption at bedtime, decreased sleep efficiency (i.e., decreased time asleep or time in bed), decreased total sleep time, and decreased sleep duration (Goldman et al., 2012; Richdale & Schreck, 2009). This includes disruptive or nondisruptive night waking. The higher prevalence of sleep disorders observed among persons with ASD appears to be partly caused by the overlap of neurobiological influences on both sleep and ASD. For example, abnormalities in GABA (an inhibitory neurotransmitter) and melatonin (a brain hormone) appear in both sleep disorders and ASD (K. P. Johnson & Malow, 2008). Disruptions in these systems can lead to poor-quality sleep and changes in the circadian sleep–wake cycles, which can appear as resistance at bedtime and sleeping at other times during the day (Durand, 2013).

Initial screening for the presence of sleep problems can occur through several sleep questionnaires, including the Pediatric Sleep Questionnaire (Chervin, Hedger, Dillon, & Pituch, 2000) and the Children's Sleep Habits Questionnaire (Owens, Spirito, & McGuinn, 2000). These allow the clinician to determine the types of sleep problems that are occurring. Once the sleep problems are identified, it is typically recommended that parents complete a sleep diary, which is designed to help them check the times when the child is asleep and awake during the day and at night. This information is used to help design interventions. If breathing problems are suspected to be involved in disrupted sleep, an overnight sleep assessment (polysomnographic evaluation) is recommended.

Research on the treatment of sleep problems in persons with ASD mainly includes studies with single subject designs (Schreck, 2001; Vriend, Corkum, Moon, & Smith, 2011). The growing numbers of these studies allow for confidence in several different interventions to assist with sleep problems, including variations of extinction, adjustment of sleep schedules, sleep restriction, and scheduled awakening (Durand, 2013). Protocols are available to help clinicians assess sleep problems and implement appropriate interventions that are designed for the specific sleep disorder and fit the needs of the family (e.g., Durand, 2008).

SUMMARY

The clinical picture of ASD is complicated by common associated disorders and difficulties. Psychiatric and medical comorbidities can add challenges to everyday activities, such as eating and sleeping, and can further test the skills of families, teachers, and others to provide help with the ASD core problems of social communication and restricted and repetitive behaviors. A growing body of research is shedding light on the assessment and treatment of many of these difficulties and supporting a more optimistic view of how to further improve the lives of those with ASD and their families.

5

Screening, Diagnosis, and Assessment

C linically evaluating children with autism spectrum disorder (ASD) is a three-level process: screening for the possible presence of ASD (Level 1); evaluation for a formal diagnosis (Level 2); and assessment of important related skills, such as adaptive behavior, motor skills, social communication, and cognitive development (Level 3). These latter aspects of evaluation are essential for developing an appropriate and comprehensive intervention plan.

EARLY SCREENING

As is described in Chapter 6, the most favorable outcomes are achieved if intervention for the symptoms of ASD begins very early in life. There is ample evidence that intensive early intervention can result in substantial gains in social and communication skills for some children with ASD

http://dx.doi.org/10.1037/14283-004
Autism Spectrum Disorder: A Clinical Guide for General Practitioners, by V. M. Durand

(Peters-Scheffer, Didden, Korzilius, & Sturmey, 2011). As a result, there is increased interest in identifying children with ASD as early as possible. Several national consensus panels (including the American Academy of Neurology, the American Psychological Society, the American Academy of Child and Adolescent Psychiatry and the American Academy of Pediatrics) recommend early screening, especially when there is parental concern or generally for all children between the ages of 18 and 24 months (Warren & Stone, 2011). The recommendation is intended to assist families with early problems and to facilitate more successful early intervention. Given the importance of early identification, some have argued that all infants should be screened for ASD (C. P. Johnson & Myers, 2007). However, there is some controversy over this proposal given that high rates of false positives (i.e., identifying children who do not have the disorder as having ASD) would substantially increase parental anxiety and could result in costly treatment for many children who do not require intensive services (Al-Qabandi, Gorter, & Rosenbaum, 2011).

Despite the availability of screening tools that will identify ASD as early as 12 to 14 months, current practices have not kept up with this development (Zwaigenbaum, 2011). For example, the average age at first diagnosis can be as late as 5 years or older in certain regions of the United States (Autism and Developmental Disabilities Monitoring Network, 2007; Pringle et al., 2012). This age is even later for children with Asperger's type ASD, averaging just over 7 years of age when initially diagnosed (Interactive Autism Network, 2010). Clinicians should be aware of the early signs of ASD and should be particularly sensitive to families reporting possible delays in their young children in areas such as social skills (e.g., eye contact, social smiling, social interest), language (e.g., delayed babbling, pointing to show others an object), play skills or visual tracking (e.g., staring at toys for long periods of time), or an insistence on a particular routine or sameness (e.g., having tantrums if toys lined up are moved even slightly). Given the odds that siblings of a child with ASD will have increased risk for ASD, close attention should be paid to development in this group. If there is concern in any of these areas, it is recommended that initial screening be completed to determine whether a more comprehensive evaluation is warranted.

Fortunately, a number of validated and easy-to-administer screening tools are available (for a comprehensive review, see Council on Children With Disabilities, 2006). Several of the most studied of these early screening tools for infants and children at both ends of the ASD continuum are described in Tables 5.1 and 5.2. Included is information on how each assessment is administered as well as information on sensitivity (i.e., the

Table 5.1

Early Screening Tools for Infants and Toddlers (Autism Spectrum Disorder, Kanner's Type)

Tool	Applicable age range	Administration	Sensitivity	Specificity
Checklist for Autism in Toddlers (Baron-Cohen, Wheelwright, et al., 2000)	18–24 months	Nine items reported by parents and five items observed by a health professional	35–38%	98%
Modified Checklist for Autism in Toddlers (Robins, Fein, Barton, & Green, 2001)	16–30 months	23-item checklist completed by caregivers	77–97%	95–99%
Early Screening of Autistic Traits Questionnaire (Dietz, Swinkels, Daalen, Engeland, & Buitelaar, 2006)	14–15 months	Two-stage screening process. Prescreening with a four-item questionnaire reported by parents and if warranted an in-home longer version (14 item; also parent report) is completed by a mental health professional.	23–88%	28–99%
Infant Toddler Checklist (Wetherby, Brosnan-Maddox, Peace, & Newton, 2008)	9–24 months	24-item checklist completed by caregiver	90–93%	90 %

(*continued*)

Table 5.1

Early Screening Tools for Infants and Toddlers
(Autism Spectrum Disorder, Kanner's Type) (*Continued*)

Tool	Applicable age range	Administration	Sensitivity	Specificity
Screening Tool for Autism in Two-Year-Olds (Stone, Coonrod, & Ousley, 2000)	24–35 months	12-item interactive screening tool; training consists of observing and scoring live and videotaped sessions, as well as receiving feedback on performance. No prior autism training is necessary.	83–95%	73%
Autism Observation Scale for Infants (Bryson, Zwaigenbaum, McDermott, Rombough, & Brian, 2008)	6–18 months	18-item direct observational measure using semistructured activities presented by trained administrators	84%	98%

average percentage of "true positives" or accurately identifying someone with ASD) and specificity (i.e., the average percentage of "true negatives" or correctly identifying that someone does not have ASD). It is generally believed that these scores should be 70% or higher to be acceptable (Barnes, 1982).

To illustrate the types of questions that are used in these screening tools, Exhibit 5.1 provides the questions from the Modified Checklist for Autism in Toddlers (M-CHAT) along with instructions on how to score parent responses.

For those suspected as having Asperger's type ASD, a small but growing number of screening tools are available. Note that the screening tools are appropriate for administration no earlier than the age of 4 because it is difficult to detect the signs of Asperger's type ASD in children younger than that (see Table 5.2).

Table 5.2

Early Screening Tools for Toddlers
(Autism Spectrum Disorder, Asperger's Type)

Tool	Applicable age range	Administration	Sensitivity	Specificity
Autism Spectrum Screening Questionnaire (Ehlers, Gillberg, & Wing, 1999)	7–16 years	27-item questionnaire completed by lay informants	62–93%	33–86%
Social Communication Questionnaire (Rutter, Bailey, & Lord, 2003)	4 years and older	Questionnaire completed by caregivers	88%	71–72%
Australian Scale for Asperger Syndrome (Rutter, Bailey, et al., 2003	5 years and older	24-item scale used as a screening tool completed by caregivers, teachers, or professionals	95%	52%
Childhood Autism Spectrum Test (Baron-Cohen, Wheelwright, et al., 2000; Scott, Baron-Cohen, Bolton, & Brayne, 2002; Williams et al., 2006)	4–11 years	37-item self-report questionnaire completed by caregivers	100%	97%

One of the early screening tools is the Childhood Autism Spectrum Test (CAST; previously called the Childhood Asperger Screening Test; Scott, Baron-Cohen, Bolton, & Brayne, 2000). The CAST can be completed by parents or teachers (see Exhibit 5.2).

The screening tools used to identify ASD early in life are simple and offer relatively simple assessments. The M-CHAT is a brief questionnaire that can be administered to parents. Although the questions themselves are relatively straightforward (e.g., "Does your child take an interest in other children?" "Does your child ever bring objects over to you [parent] to show you something?"), it is recommended that a follow-up interview be conducted to help clarify the responses and reduce to number of false positives (Yama, Freeman, Graves, Yuan, & Campbell, 2012).

Exhibit 5.1

Questions on the Modified Checklist for Autism in Toddlers

Please fill out the following about how your child usually is. Please try to answer every question. If the behavior is rare (e.g., you've seen it once or twice), please answer as if the child does not do it.

1. Does your child enjoy being swung, bounced on your knee, etc.?   Yes   No

2. Does your child take an interest in other children?   Yes   No

3. Does your child like climbing on things, such as up stairs?   Yes   No

4. Does your child enjoy playing peek-a-boo/ hide-and-seek?   Yes   No

5. Does your child ever pretend, for example, to talk on the phone or take care of a doll or pretend other things?   Yes   No

6. Does your child ever use his/her index finger to point, to ask for something?   Yes   No

7. Does your child ever use his/her index finger to point, to indicate interest in something?   Yes   No

8. Can your child play properly with small toys (e.g. cars or blocks) without just mouthing, fiddling, or dropping them?   Yes   No

9. Does your child ever bring objects over to you (parent) to show you something?   Yes   No

10. Does your child look you in the eye for more than a second or two?   Yes   No

11. Does your child ever seem oversensitive to noise? (e.g., plugging ears)   Yes   No

12. Does your child smile in response to your face or your smile?   Yes   No

Exhibit 5.1

Questions on the Modified Checklist for Autism in Toddlers (*Continued*)

13.	Does your child imitate you? (e.g., you make a face-will your child imitate it?)	Yes	No
14.	Does your child respond to his/her name when you call?	Yes	No
15.	If you point at a toy across the room, does your child look at it?	Yes	No
16.	Does your child walk?	Yes	No
17.	Does your child look at things you are looking at?	Yes	No
18.	Does your child make unusual finger movements near his/her face?	Yes	No
19.	Does your child try to attract your attention to his/her own activity?	Yes	No
20.	Have you ever wondered if your child is deaf?	Yes	No
21.	Does your child understand what people say?	Yes	No
22.	Does your child sometimes stare at nothing or wander with no purpose?	Yes	No
23.	Does your child look at your face to check your reaction when faced with something unfamiliar?	Yes	No

Note. Further information is available from http://www.autismspeaks.org/what-autism/diagnosis/m-chat. Scoring instructions are available from the authors (http://www2.gsu.edu/~psydlr/DianaLRobins/Official_M-CHAT_Website_files/M-CHAT_score_rev.pdf). Children who fail the checklist should be evaluated in more depth by the clinician or referred for a developmental evaluation with a specialist (Robins et al., 2001). From "The Modified Checklist for Autism in Toddlers: An Initial Study Investigating the Early Detection of Autism and Pervasive Developmental Disorders," by Robins, D. L., Fein, D., Barton, M. L., and Green, J. A., 2001, *Journal of Autism and Developmental Disorders, 31*, p. 142. Retrieved from http://www2.gsu.edu/~psydlr/DianaLRobins/Official_M-CHAT_Website.html. Copyright 1999 by Diana Robins, Deborah Fein, and Marianne Barton. Reprinted with permission.

Exhibit 5.2		

The Childhood Autism Spectrum Test

1. Does s/he join in playing games with other children easily?	Yes	No
2. Does s/he come up to you spontaneously for a chat?	Yes	No
3. Was s/he speaking by 2 years old?	Yes	No
4. Does s/he enjoy sports?	Yes	No
5. Is it important to him/her to fit in with the peer group?	Yes	No
6. Does s/he appear to notice unusual details that others miss?	Yes	No
7. Does s/he tend to take things literally?	Yes	No
8. When s/he was 3 years old, did s/he spend a lot of time pretending (e.g., play-acting being a superhero, or holding teddy's tea parties)?	Yes	No
9. Does s/he like to do things over and over again, in the same way all the time?	Yes	No
10. Does s/he find it easy to interact with other children?	Yes	No
11. Can s/he keep a two-way conversation going?	Yes	No
12. Can s/he read appropriately for his/her age?	Yes	No
13. Does s/he mostly have the same interests as his/her peers?	Yes	No
14. Does s/he have an interest which takes up so much time that s/he does little else?	Yes	No
15. Does s/he have friends, rather than just acquaintances?	Yes	No
16. Does s/he often bring you things s/he is interested in to show you?	Yes	No
17. Does s/he enjoy joking around?	Yes	No
18. Does s/he have difficulty understanding the rules for polite behaviour?	Yes	No

Exhibit 5.2

The Childhood Autism Spectrum Test (*Continued*)

19. Does s/he appear to have an unusual memory for details? Yes No

20. Is his/her voice unusual (e.g., overly adult, flat, or very monotonous)? Yes No

21. Are people important to him/her? Yes No

22. Can s/he dress him/herself? Yes No

23. Is s/he good at turn-taking in conversation? Yes No

24. Does s/he play imaginatively with other children, and engage in role-play? Yes No

25. Does s/he often do or say things that are tactless or socially inappropriate? Yes No

26. Can s/he count to 50 without leaving out any numbers? Yes No

27. Does s/he make normal eye-contact? Yes No

28. Does s/he have any unusual and repetitive movements? Yes No

29. Is his/her social behaviour very one-sided and always on his/her own terms? Yes No

30. Does s/he sometimes say "you" or "s/he" when s/he means "I"? Yes No

31. Does s/he prefer imaginative activities such as play-acting or story-telling, rather than numbers or lists of facts? Yes No

32. Does s/he sometimes lose the listener because of not explaining what s/he is talking about? Yes No

33. Can s/he ride a bicycle (even if with stabilisers)? Yes No

34. Does s/he try to impose routines on him/herself, or on others, in such a way that it causes problems? Yes No

(*continued*)

Exhibit 5.2

The Childhood Autism Spectrum Test (*Continued*)

35. Does s/he care how s/he is perceived by the rest of the group?   Yes   No

36. Does s/he often turn conversations to his/her favourite subject rather than following what the other person wants to talk about?   Yes   No

37. Does s/he have odd or unusual phrases?   Yes   No

Note. The scoring instructions are as follows: Score "1" if the respondent answers "No" to questions 1, 2, 5, 8, 10, 11, 13, 15, 16, 17, 21, 23, 24, 27, 31, and 35. Score "1" if the respondent answers "Yes" to questions 6, 7, 9, 14, 18, 19, 20, 25, 28, 29, 30, 32, 34, 36, and 37. Sum all "1's" to get a total score. Maximum score possible is 31, cut-off currently is 15 for possible autism syndrome disorder or related social-communication difficulties. Questions that are not scored are controls. From "The CAST (Childhood Asperger Syndrome Test): Preliminary Development of UK Screen for Mainstream Primary-School Children," by F. Scott, S. Baron-Cohen, P. Bolton, and C. Brayne, 2002, *Autism, 6,* pp. 6–31. Retrieved from http://www.autismresearchcentre.com/arc_tests. Copyright 2002 University of Cambridge. Reprinted with permission.

DIAGNOSIS

If screening suggests the possible presence of ASD, standardized diagnostic assessments are available to confirm the diagnosis. Some of these instruments (see Table 5.3) are more elaborate forms of the screening tools described and are completed by caregivers. In addition, semistructured interviews and observational measures allow for more detailed information. Some of the more frequently used measures are included here (see Table 5.3). Although questionnaires such as the Social Responsiveness Scale (Constantino & Gruber, 2002) can be completed by caregivers or teachers and can be easily scored, a diagnosis of ASD should be made by an experienced clinician (Steiner, Goldsmith, Snow, & Chawarska, 2012) because the consequences of having this diagnosis in terms of prognosis and treatment are significant. At the present time, the Autism Diagnostic Observation Schedule (Lord et al., 2000) is considered the instrument of choice (often referred to as the gold standard); it requires extensive training in its use and interpretation.

Table 5.3

Diagnostic Assessment of Autism Spectrum Disorder (Kanner's Type)

Tool type	Diagnostic assessment	Administration
Questionnaires	Autism Behavior Checklist (Krug, Arick, & Almond, 1980)	57-item checklist completed by teachers
	Gilliam Autism Rating (Gilliam, 1995)	56-item questionnaire divided into four 14-item subscales completed by caregivers
	Social Communication Questionnaire (Rutter, Bailey, et al., 2003)	40-item screening questionnaire completed by caregivers
	Social Responsiveness Scale (Constantino & Gruber, 2002)	65-item questionnaire completed by caregivers or teachers
Semistructured interviews	Autism Diagnostic Interview–Revised (ADI–R; Rutter, Le Couteur, & Lord, 2003)	A standardized, semistructured diagnostic interview for use with caregivers administered by trained examiners; examiners must have prior education, training, and experience with autism spectrum disorder and pervasive developmental disorder, complete clinical training equivalent to 12–18 hours of professional continuing education credit, and practice using the ADI–R on informal evaluations; if the ADI–R will be used in formal research the examiner must complete an additional research training workshop and exercises to exhibit accuracy and understanding of ADI–R coding
	Diagnostic Interview for Social and Communicative Disorders (Wing, Leekam, Libby, Gould, & Larcombe, 2002)	Investigator based semistructured interview reported by caregivers
Observational measures	Childhood Autism Rating Scale (Schopler, Reichler, & Renner, 1986)	Behavior observation scale of 15 items rated by trained observer

(continued)

Table 5.3

Diagnostic Assessment of Autism Spectrum Disorder (Kanner's Type) (*Continued*)

Tool type	Diagnostic assessment	Administration
	Autism Diagnostic Observation Schedule (ADOS; Lord et al., 2000)	Series of structured and semistructured presses for interaction presented, videotaped, and coded by a trained examiner; examiners must have prior education, training, and experience with autism spectrum disorder and pervasive development disorder, complete clinical training equivalent to 12–18 hours of professional continuing education credit, and practice using the ADOS on informal evaluations; if the ADOS will be used in formal research the examiner must complete an additional research training workshop and exercises to exhibit accuracy and understanding of ADOS coding.

A few diagnostic instruments are specifically aimed at persons with Asperger's type ASD; two are noted in Table 5.4. Several of the diagnostic instruments (e.g., Autism Diagnostic Observation Schedule) can be used to diagnose persons at this end of the autism spectrum as well. Note that one of these assessments, the Autism Spectrum Quotient (Baron-Cohen, Wheelwright, et al., 2000), is a self-report measure and allows for adults with average or above IQ scores to identify behaviors and traits that may indicate Asperger's type ASD.

Table 5.4

Diagnostic Questionnaires Used to Assess Autism Spectrum Disorder (Asperger's Type)

Diagnostic assessment	Administration
Autism Spectrum Quotient (Baron-Cohen, Wheelwright, et al., 2000)	50-item self-report questionnaire
Autism Spectrum Screening Questionnaire (Ehlers et al., 1999)	27-item questionnaire completed by lay informants, requires no prior training to administer

---

Clinical Concerns: Diagnostic Reliability

Differential diagnosis for ASD seems on the surface to be relatively straightforward. However, research points to wide variations in diagnoses of those with ASD (Sharma, Woolfson, & Hunter, 2012). In one study of more than 2,100 children ages 4 to 18, diagnoses varied by location, even when the same diagnostic method was used (Lord, Petkova, et al., 2012). One interpretation of this variability is that the presence of services for different types of disorders (e.g., an excellent program for children with ASD) play a role in the type of diagnosis received. In other words, the desire for more intensive intervention (e.g., a higher teacher-to-student ratio, better trained teachers) may cause clinicians to make the diagnosis for a child who may be on the margin of having ASD. Also, pressure from families and educational programs may unduly influence these decisions, and clinicians should be wary of this phenomenon.

ASSESSMENT

Assessment for ASD focuses on a number of areas across several domains of concern (Steiner et al., 2012). Guidelines are available to direct the assessment process (see, e.g., American Academy of Pediatrics, 2007; C. P. Johnson & Myers, 2007) and ASD diagnostic centers can be found by contacting sites through the Autism Treatment Network (see http://www.autismspeaks.org/science/resources-programs/autism-treatment-network).

Typically a multidisciplinary team will conduct assessments in areas such as social communication, cognitive development, adaptive behavior, and health concerns and screen for unusual motor skills or sensory behaviors. In addition, specific assessments are completed if the person exhibits a variety of disruptive behaviors. Assessments are warranted for any comorbid conditions (e.g., anxiety, sleep problems, attention-deficit/hyperactivity disorder; see Chapter 4) that may have an impact on present and future development. Multiple informants are used (e.g., parents, teachers, self-report, clinical observations) given the high potential for discrepancy with only one source of assessment information (Jepsen, Gray, & Taffe, 2012). A complete review of the full range of assessment instruments that can be used for persons with ASD is beyond the scope of this guide, but the more commonly administered tools are described.

Intellectual Assessment

Assessment of intellectual functioning is essential in ASD because level of cognitive functioning is correlated with level of adaptive behavior, severity of symptoms, and outcome (Filipek et al., 1999). By definition, individuals with ASD of the Asperger's type will score in the average or above average range on IQ tests. They do not have significant delays in language or cognitive development but may score higher on verbal scales than on performance scales, and this should be considered in treatment planning (e.g., implications for academic performance). Those with Kanner's type ASD may score lower on IQ tests. However, these results must be interpreted with care. Because individuals with ASD (especially of the Kanner's type) tend not to have significant social motivation, they may not perform at optimal levels on these tests. In other words, they may not put in significant effort to please parents or teachers with their performance on such tests. Some research shows that enhancing motivation to perform optimally (e.g., taking the test in a favorite corner, providing short breaks for perseverance) can improve scores significantly in this population (L. K. Koegel, Koegel, & Smith, 1997). Care obviously needs to be taken to avoid varying too much from the standardized administration protocol such that it invalidates the results.

Commonly administered intelligence tests used with individuals who are sufficiently verbal include the Wechsler Intelligence Scales (e.g., Wechsler Preschool and Primary Scale of Intelligence—III; Wechsler Intelligence Scale for Children—IV; Wechsler Adult Intelligence Scale—IV; Wechsler, 2002, 2003, 2008) and the Stanford–Binet Intelligence Scales (Roid, 2003). A variety of intelligence tests are available for individuals with more limited communication skills. The Kaufman Assessment Battery for Children, Second Edition (A. S. Kaufman & Kaufman, 2003) is applicable for children from ages 2½ to 12½ but requires that they have some receptive language ability. The Leiter International Performance Scale—Revised is a completely nonverbal test (appropriate for individuals ages 2–21) and may be best for those with very limited skills (Leiter, 2002). The Mullen Scales of Early Learning is designed for very young children (ages 1–42 months) and assesses skill in areas including gross motor, visual reception, fine motor, receptive language, and expressive language (Mullen, 1997).

Social Communication Assessment

Typically, the diagnostic assessment process in persons with ASD identifies deficits in social communication skills. For example, the Autism Diagnostic Observation Schedule described previously includes multiple assessments of a variety of social skills (e.g., presence of joint attention, initiations and response to initiations). However, because responses to social situations vary so widely from person to person and from setting to setting, more specific information is often required for treatment planning (Murray, Ruble, Willis, & Molloy, 2009). One tool specifically designed to assess social functioning in persons with Asperger's type ASD is the Vanderbilt Treatment and Research Institute for Autism Spectrum Disorders (TRIAD) Social Skills Assessment (Stone, Ruble, Coonrod, Hepburn, & Pennington, 2003). This multi-informant tool assesses four areas of social development: (a) ability to understand emotions and perspectives of others, (b) ability to initiate interactions, (c) ability to maintain interactions, and (d) ability to respond to others. The use of multiple informants was shown to be valuable in the initial study because teachers and parents did not always agree on competencies for specific social behaviors, perhaps as a result of observing the child in differing social situations. This kind of assessment is always supplemented by observations by experienced professionals of the person in naturally occurring social situations.

Language assessment is important because language ability is predictive of long-term outcomes (Howlin, 2005). For those with existing verbal language abilities, the verbal scales of an IQ test often provide useful information about the person's capabilities. In addition, other instruments can be used to further assess receptive vocabulary skills (e.g., Peabody Picture Vocabulary Test—Third Edition; Dunn & Dunn, 1997) and expressive vocabulary abilities (e.g., Expressive One-Word Picture Vocabulary

Test; Brownell, 2000). Individuals with ASD are often limited in the area of *pragmatic communication,* or the use of social communication skills such as body language and understanding the intentions of others, and assessments for this specific set of skills exist as well (e.g., Communication and Symbolic Behavior Scales; Wetherby & Prizant, 2002). All of this information is compiled and used by the interdisciplinary team along with input from a speech-language pathologist to help design appropriate intervention plans.

Adaptive Behavior Assessment

Adaptive functioning refers to how effectively individuals cope with common life demands and how well they meet the standards of personal independence expected of someone in their age group, sociocultural background, and community setting. The Vineland Adaptive Behavior Scales, Second Edition (Sparrow, Cicchetti, & Balla, 2005) is one of the most widely used instruments and assesses communication, daily living skills, socialization, motor skills, and maladaptive behavior. As with intellectual assessment, consideration should be given to the suitability of the instrument to the child's sociocultural background, education, associated limitations, motivation, and cooperation.

Challenging Behavior Assessment

Two types of assessment strategies are used with problem or challenging behaviors, such as aggression, tantrums, self-injury, or repetitive behaviors. The first step is to identify those behaviors that are most disruptive at home, in school, or in community settings. Although behavior scales created for typically developing children, such as the Child Behavior Checklist (Achenbach & Edelbrock, 1991), the Preschool Behavior Questionnaire (Behar & Stringfield, 1974), and the Conners' Rating Scales–3rd Edition (Conners, 2008) have been used with children and adolescents with Asperger's type ASD, the measures may be insensitive and inappropriate for assessment of individuals with Kanner's type ASD. The Developmental Behavior Checklist (Einfeld & Tonge, 1989), an adaptation of the Child Behavior Checklist, includes items more specific to children with ASD. Other scales appropriate for use with this population include the Behavior

Problem Inventory (Rojahn, Matson, Lott, Esbensen, & Smalls, 2001), the Aberrant Behavior Checklist (Aman, Tasse, Rojahn, & Hammer, 1996), and the Nisonger Child Behavior Rating Form (Aman et al., 1996).

The second stage of assessment that is essential for developing appropriate behavioral interventions is to determine the function of a problem behavior (Durand, 1990); in other words, the goal is to assess what might be causing the behavior to persist (e.g., to gain attention from others, to escape unpleasant situations). There are different forms of functional assessment, and to improve the accuracy of assessment results, it is typically recommended that multiple forms of assessment be used. A number of strategies can be useful for determining the function of behavior, including informal observations, antecedent behavior–consequence charts, functional analyses, and rating scales. A functional analysis— manipulating aspects of the environment to assess behavior change—is frequently cited as the best method of determining the function of a behavior problem (Hanley, Iwata, & McCord, 2003); however, this can often be difficult to conduct in typical settings. A number of assessment instruments are available to provide additional information about the functions of behavior, including the Motivation Assessment Scale (Durand & Crimmins, 1988), the Functional Analysis Interview Form (O'Neill, Horner, Albin, Storey, & Sprague, 1990), and the Questions About Behavioral Function (Paclawskyj, Matson, Rush, Smalls, & Vollmer, 2000). These types of instruments can be used to provide additional and convergent information about behavioral functions, which in turn can be used to determine appropriate interventions (see Chapter 6).

SUMMARY

Screening, diagnosis, and assessment of ASD require considerable clinical skill and expertise and should involve family members as well as professionals from related fields. Advances in the ability to identify ASD of the Kanner's type in very young children are likely to help many children make substantial progress with early intervention. As assessments evolve, interventions can be more prescriptive and targeted to the skills needed by the individual.

6

Treatment

Unlike major depressive disorder or the anxiety disorders, no single intervention is applied unilaterally to treat persons with autism spectrum disorder (ASD). Rather, intervention is focused on specific deficits (and strengths). The general categories of difficulties—social communication and behavioral challenges—are assessed (as described in Chapter 5), and interventions are individually tailored as needed. In addition, when assessments identify other areas of need (e.g., cognitive impairments), these too are integrated into a comprehensive intervention plan. The overall goals include maximizing the independence and quality of life of the person with ASD and supporting family members (National Research Council, 2001).

The foundation of most interventions for ASD is educational. Behavioral and other rehabilitative strategies are used to teach necessary skills and to help reduce the frequency and intensity of problem behaviors.

http://dx.doi.org/10.1037/14283-005
Autism Spectrum Disorder: A Clinical Guide for General Practitioners, by V. M. Durand

Most current medical interventions are palliative (i.e., are meant to reduce symptoms such as anxiety or irritability) or are designed to manage associated problems such as sleep disorders or seizures. To date, there are no medical interventions that have been demonstrated to correct the central problems of social communication deficits and restricted and repetitive behaviors (Carrasco, Volkmar, & Bloch, 2012; Siegel & Beaulieu, 2012).

This chapter presents the range of evidence-based interventions used with clients who have ASD, along with the types of skills and training necessary to carry out these treatments.[1] Highlighted are interventions for the core symptoms of ASD as well as early intervention approaches that are designed to avoid the derailment of important developmental milestones. These are combined with interventions for comorbid difficulties that can interfere with efforts to teach social communication and reduce problem behaviors (see Chapter 4). Because interventions for individuals on either end of the autism spectrum (i.e., those with Kanner's type ASD and Asperger's type ASD) vary considerably (even though the categories of difficulties are the same), the chapter separates out the treatments for these two general groups. Clinicians should be aware, however, of the vast heterogeneity of needs even within these two groups; individualized plans are always recommended.

INTERVENTION FOR KANNER'S TYPE ASD

It is important to distinguish between individual techniques that are validated ways of teaching specific skills to those with ASD and more comprehensive programs or packages of interventions designed to address one or more of the core symptoms and associated concerns. The intervention literature was reviewed by two projects with slightly different perspectives: the National Professional Development Center on Autism Spectrum Disorders (a multi-university center that promotes the use of evidence-based practice for children and adolescents with ASD) and the

---

[1] Note that there are many complementary and alternative approaches that lack a strong evidence base; readers can find a description of many of these on the website Autism Speaks (http://www.autismspeaks.org/what-autism/treatment/complementary-treatments-autism).

National Standards Project (a report compiled by the National Autism Center with input by experts in the field that provides information about which treatments have been shown to be effective for individuals with ASD). Their findings are summarized in Figure 6.1. This figure outlines the variety of techniques and packages that have a significant evidence base. It should be noted that other reviews that exclude studies with single subject designs rate some of these approaches as having low to moderate strength of evidence (Maglione, Gans, Das, Timbie, & Kasari, 2012). However, the data in this area are developing rapidly, and definitive statements about some of these approaches may be premature.

A number of evidence-based techniques are derived from the field of applied behavior analysis and have been proven to successfully teach individual behaviors to persons with ASD. Early efforts to teach basic social communication and reduce problem behaviors relied on a format referred to as *discrete trial training* (T. Smith, 2001; Wilczynski, Rue, Hunter, & Christian, 2012). This involves one-to-one intervention using learning trials that have a specified beginning and end. Usually seated across from a teacher, the student is presented with repeated trials on the same skill (e.g., "Touch your nose") until mastery is achieved. Other evidence-based teaching components that are incorporated into this method of teaching skills include prompting, antecedent-based intervention, time delay, reinforcement, task analysis, response interruption/redirection, and differential reinforcement. Properly designing intervention plans using these techniques and subsequently carrying out these procedures require significant training in applied behavior analysis (Wilczynski et al., 2012). When applying these techniques to students with ASD, it is necessary that those involved are fully trained in the nature of the disorder and its many manifestations.

At some level, most educational interventions for ASD include aspects of discrete trial training. However, therapists who rely solely on this approach and apply it only in highly structured settings should be aware of the limitations. High levels of structure and teaching in artificial settings without peers may provide an obstacle to assisting these individuals in becoming more social. In addition, students may not use the skills

Evidence-Based Practices Identified by the National Professional Development Center (NPDC) on ASD	Established Treatments Identified by the National Standards Project (NSP)										
	Antecedent Package	Behavioral Package	Story-based Intervention Package	Modeling	Naturalistic Teaching Strategies	Peer Training Package	Pivotal Response Treatment	Schedules	Self-Management	Comprehensive Behavioral Treatment for Young Children	Joint Attention Intervention
Prompting	X									The NPDC on ASD did not review comprehensive treatment models. Components of The Comprehensive Behavioral Treatment of Young Children overlap with many NPDC-identified practices.	The NPDC on ASD considers joint attention to be an outcome rather than an intervention. Components of joint attention interventions overlap with many NPDC-identified practices.
Antecedent-Based Intervention	X			X							
Time delay	X										
Reinforcement		X									
Task analysis		X									
Discrete Trial Training		X									
Functional Behavior Analysis		X									
Functional Communication Training		X									
Response Interruption/Redirection		X									
Differential Reinforcement		X									
Social Narratives			X								
Video Modeling				X							
Naturalistic Interventions					X						
Peer Mediated Intervention						X					
Pivotal Response Training							X				
Visual Supports								X			
Structured Work Systems								X			
Self-Management									X		
Parent Implemented Intervention	The NSP did not consider parent-implemented intervention as a category of evidence-based practice. However, 24 of the studies reviewed by the NSP under other intervention categories involve parents implementing the intervention.										
Social Skills Training Groups	Social Skills Training Groups (Social Skills Package) was identified as an emerging practice by NSP.										
Speech Generating Devices	Speech Generating Devices (Augmentative and Alternative Communication Device) was identified as an emerging practice by the NSP.										
Computer Aided Instruction	Computer Aided Instruction (Technology-based Treatment) was identified as an emerging practice by the NSP.										
Picture Exchange Communication	Picture Exchange Communication System was identified as an emerging practice by the NSP.										
Extinction	Extinction (Reductive Package) was identified as an emerging practice by the NSP.										

Figure 6.1

Overlap between evidence-based practices identified by the National Professional Development Center on Autism Spectrum Disorders and the National Standards Project. From *Overlap Between Evidence-Based Practices Identified by the National Professional Development Center on Autism Spectrum Disorders and the National Standards Project*, by National Professional Development Center on Autism Spectrum Disorders, 2011. Retrieved from http://autismpdc.fpg.unc.edu/content/national-standards-project. Copyright 2011 by Frank Porter Graham Child Development Institute, University of North Carolina at Chapel Hill. Reprinted with permission.

taught in these highly structured sessions outside of the one-to-one setting (Ingersoll, 2010). More recently, several different approaches have normalized this type of teaching by bringing the instruction away from a desk with one child and one teacher to regular settings at home, in school, and in the community; these approaches use more child-directed versus adult-directed techniques (naturalistic teaching strategies). The next section discusses different applications of evidence-based practices when teaching social communication skills and when attempting to reduce challenging behaviors (e.g., aggression, tantrums, self-injury).

Teaching Social Communication Skills

One of the more extensively studied areas involves interventions aimed at teaching individuals with the Kanner's type ASD how to communicate with and relate to others in a meaningful way. Many of these individuals have no speech at all, whereas others may have idiosyncratic speech (e.g., echolalia) or communicate simple requests in one or two word phrases (e.g., "Cookie please"). The goal is to give each person with ASD the skills necessary to make their wants and needs understood by others; the optimal goal is to be able to communicate in a social way. Research on improving social communication skills usually focuses on (a) the type of skills that are targeted (e.g., teaching requests, improving joint attention), (b) the method of teaching communication (e.g., incidental teaching, using peer-mediated learning, social stories), (c) the modality of social communication (e.g., speech, augmentative and alternative communication strategies), and (d) comprehensive treatment packages that target overall improvement in ASD symptoms and daily functioning.

The types of skills to be taught are determined through the comprehensive assessment conducted prior to intervention, with a consideration of both the level of skills the student already possesses (e.g., has some verbal ability vs. has no functional communication skills) and the immediate and long-term priorities for the student. Attempts to teach children with ASD to make requests for desired objects (e.g., "Soda please") or activities (e.g., "I want outside") are often more successful than efforts to teach communication skills that are socially motivated (H. Goldstein, 2002). For example, saying "hello" to someone usually leads to some form of social acknowledgement by the other person (e.g., "Hi! How are you?"). However, if a person has limited interest in social interaction, or if these interactions are anxiety producing, this everyday exchange will probably not be attempted given that the consequence (social attention) is not reinforcing. This was the case with Maria, who was able to quickly learn how to point to pictures that illustrated some of her favorite activities, such as drinking, playing in the play corner, and going outside. However, when her teachers attempted to get her to point appropriately to a picture that signified greetings, for example, they were not successful in getting her to reliably use this picture in the appropriate context. Presumably, Maria did not enjoy social interactions and therefore was not motivated to learn these types of social communication.

Researchers in the field often pair a preferred nonsocial consequence (e.g., getting a favorite food) with the social consequence to improve the chances that the child will engage in more social communication strategies. However, without a natural interest in continued social interactions with others, it is difficult to maintain this type of social communicative exchange in those with Kanner's type ASD. This remains one of the continuing clinical challenges in the field. As described later, efforts at early intervention with this population attempt to address this lack of social motivation in order to improve later attempts to teach important social communication skills.

A number of evidence-based strategies for teaching social communication skills exist and, again, often depend on the needs and skills of the learner. When the goal of social communication is through the use of speech, the techniques described previously in the discussion on discrete trial training are used to teach beginning labeling and requests, progressing to the use of sentences. Several adaptations to this approach involve more "naturalistic" techniques that include arranging the environment so that the child initiates an interest (e.g., placing a favorite toy just out of reach), and this is used as a teaching opportunity (e.g., giving the child the instruction to say, "I want truck"). Various evidence-based treatment packages use aspects of this approach, including incidental teaching (McGee, Morrier,

& Daly, 1999), pivotal response training (R. Koegel & Koegel, 2012), and milieu teaching (Hancock & Kaiser, 2012). These techniques have been demonstrated to increase a variety of social communication skills (e.g., making requests, interactions with peers, joint attention skills, play skills) among some children with Kanner's type ASD (H. Goldstein, 2002).

Other approaches to teaching social communication skills use techniques that exploit the tendency of persons with ASD to learn skills better through visual than verbal cues. For example, variations of video modeling have been used to show students with ASD how to behave and interact in a variety of social communication situations (Bellini & Akullian, 2007; Buggey, 2012; Charlop-Christy, Le, & Freeman, 2000; Nikopoulos & Keenan, 2004). In addition, the use of visually based stories that students can use as cues in social situations (called *social narratives*) has proven successful when teaching appropriate behavior in these scenarios (e.g., how to wait in line in the cafeteria; Odom, Collet-Klingenberg, Rogers, & Hatton, 2010; Test, Richter, Knight, & Spooner, 2011). The stories may include pictures or other visual aids that guide learners toward appropriate behaviors and responses. In addition to relying on teachers to instruct students on these new communication skills, some work points to advantages for peer-mediated strategies (using same-age, typically developing peers as tutors or models) as well as employing parents and siblings as instructors.

Approximately 25% of individuals with ASD do not develop speech proficiency sufficient to communicate their needs effectively (D. K. Anderson et al., 2007). For children with limited or no verbal abilities, a variety of alternative communicative methods are used. These methods include manual sign language, graphic symbols, and speech-generating devices. Early research using basic sign language demonstrated that some children without functional speech could learn to communicate with manual gestures (often with speech prompts included; e.g., Carr, 1979; Carr, Binkoff, Kologinsky, & Eddy, 1978). However, there are problems with relying on this form of communication. For example, the signs generated by a student with ASD may not be performed clearly and can become idiosyncratic to that individual and therefore difficult to interpret. In addition, the use of sign language with those who do not understand it can result in significant frustration (Mirenda & Iacono, 2009).

The use of graphic symbols (e.g., pictures of desired items or activities) to encourage communication has an emerging research base; symbols are used as visual aids for monitoring school and home schedules (e.g., visual supports), as a means of letting students make choices (e.g., pointing to one of a series of activity options), and for general expressive communication (Wegner, 2012). A variation of this approach, the picture exchange communication system, teaches students to select one or more pictures or words and hand them to another person (Bondy & Frost, 1994; Tincani & Devis, 2011). The potential advantage of this approach is that the student can initiate communication with someone even if the other person's attention is focused elsewhere.

A related approach uses speech generating devices to assist nonverbal students in communicating with others (J. B. Ganz et al., 2012). A variety of devices are available that can be programmed to generate human speech when a picture or word is pressed by the student (e.g., "Help me"); this has the advantage of being able to catch the attention of others as well as being understood by anyone. With advancing technologies and available software that can be used to easily program these devices (e.g., tablet computers), their use is increasing. Some research suggests that students with ASD may have idiosyncratic preferences for one system over another (e.g., picture exchange communication system vs. speech generating devices; van der Meer, Sutherland, O'Reilly, Lancioni, & Sigafoos, 2012), and therefore the selection of any of these nonspeech approaches to teaching social communication should be guided in part by student choice.

Treatment for Challenging Behavior

A significant evidence base exists for the treatment of challenging behaviors in Kanner's type ASD (Durand, 2012). As with interventions for social communicative behaviors, interventions for challenging behavior rely mainly on techniques derived from applied behavior analysis. The general strategy involves assessing the function of the behavior (called *functional behavior assessment*) and using a variety of techniques to support appropriate behavior and teach alternative behaviors. It is important to note that the repetitive behaviors of those with ASD (e.g., stereotyped movements, repetitive manipulation of objects, some self-injurious behaviors) remain a challenge for intervention efforts, and the database for effective interventions is limited (Boyd, McDonough, & Bodfish, 2012). These behaviors may be more intractable because they may involve internal processes related to sensory activities. Some research suggests that some of these repetitive behaviors can be later used by these individuals to manipulate their environment (Durand & Carr, 1987). In other words, these individuals learn that some of these behaviors may lead others to back away (e.g., teachers may stop providing task demands), or they may find that others will attend to them and learn to engage in these behaviors to get social attention.

The evidence-based practices for more socially based behavior problems, such as aggression, some self-injurious behavior, and tantrums, include the components mentioned previously, such as reinforcement and prompting for appropriate behaviors. More formal processes, such as functional behavior assessments, are used to assess the functions of these behaviors. When the functions are determined, alternative behaviors are often taught (called *functional communication training*). This technique was used for Maria for her tantrums at home and in the classroom. Through a functional behavioral assessment (which included interviews with her parents and her teachers and observations in her classroom), it was determined that most of her challenging behaviors occurred to enable her to escape from unpleasant situations such as difficult tasks. Thus, she was taught to point to a picture of a break area in the classroom where she could take a 5-minute break from her work. Maria quickly learned that after working for a period of time and when the teacher presented her with an opportunity to take a break, she could use the break area to briefly escape from a difficult situation. Over time, the number of tantrums dramatically diminished at school and at home. Numerous studies have documented the effectiveness of functional communication training to significantly reduce a range of challenging behavior in this population, including aggression, self-injurious behavior, tantrums, and wandering (Durand, 1990, 2012; Lang et al., 2009).

Comprehensive Treatment Packages

Many comprehensive treatment packages are used with those having Kanner's type ASD; typically, they are implemented either in schools or in special clinical settings (Howlin, Magiati, & Charman, 2009; Maglione et al., 2012; Odom, Boyd, Hall, & Hume, 2010; Peters-Scheffer et al., 2011; Reichow & Wolery, 2009; S. J. Rogers & Vismara, 2008). Most of these programs involve parents or other caregivers in order to extend teaching into the home and community. There is a general consensus that for treatment to be optimally successful it should be carried out for a minimum of 25 hours per week for a whole year (National Research Council, 2001). This is just a general guideline; the specific interventions and their level of intensity are determined individually according to the needs of the person (Wilczynski et al., 2012).

The comprehensive programs with some empirical support can be broadly divided into three categories: (a) behavioral programs using applied behavior analysis techniques, (b) behavioral programs that integrate developmental considerations to guide treatment targets, and (c) programs that have a relationship-based focus (Maglione et al., 2012; Odom, Boyd, et al., 2010).[2] In their review of 30 comprehensive program models, Odom, Boyd, et al. (2010) evaluated these models[3] on the basis of several criteria, including thorough documentation of their procedures, data on the fidelity of implementation, outcome data, and the availability of independent replications of the program. Some—Autism Partnerships, CARD, Children's Toddler Program, DIR, Denver, Douglass, LEAP, Lovaas Institute, May Institute, PCDI, PRT, Responsive Teaching, SCERTS, and TEACCH—scored highly on several of these measures. Others—Eden, Hanen, Higashi, Lancaster, Son Rise, and Summit—did not receive high ratings in most of the categories. It is important to note again that research evaluating techniques and programs for students with ASD is evolving rapidly, and several of these programs are currently being studied in recent and ongoing randomized clinical trials (e.g., G. Dawson et al., 2010).

---

[2] A brief description of each of these programs can be found in the glossary.

[3] Many of these models are "brand-named," often according to the center or university associated with the programs.

Clinical Concerns: Appropriate Educational Settings

One long-standing controversy in the field of ASD relates to the types of settings that are best for educating students with ASD. Many schools provide separate classes for them in order to provide specialized and sometimes more intensive intervention (e.g., more teachers per student). These students have different teaching needs, and therefore instructors need to be specially trained (especially for those with the more "classic" type of ASD). However, segregated classrooms have often been criticized because they isolate students with ASD from their peers (e.g., Durand, 2005; Simpson, de Boer-Ott, & Smith-Myles, 2003).

One controversial report compared children with ASD who were not educated in an inclusive setting with children having ASD who spent no less than 75% of their time in a general education classroom (Foster & Pearson, 2012). The researchers reported no differences between the groups in their likelihood to attend college or drop out of high school or in their functional cognitive score. Unfortunately, this study did not evaluate the quality of instruction or the training of instructors. Clearly, merely placing students in inclusive settings without support will not result in meaningful results. However, model programs exist that successfully include students with a broad range of abilities (e.g., McGee et al., 1999; Stahmer & Ingersoll, 2004). More comprehensive research that looks at the factors that contribute to successful inclusion with meaningful outcomes is sorely needed. Until then, clinicians can advise parents that the most important aspects of an educational environment for children with ASD are the level of training of the educators and related professionals (e.g., speech therapists, occupational therapists) and the program's use of evidence-based practices. Autism program quality indicators have been developed that can be used to assist parents when evaluating a particular school-based program (Crimmins, Durand, Theurer-Kaufman, & Everett, 2001).

Early Intensive Behavioral Intervention

In 1987, a landmark (and highly controversial) study by Ivar Lovaas at UCLA reported on the effects of using intensive intervention techniques from applied behavior analysis with children with ASD who were younger than age 3½ years (Lovaas, 1987). This intervention (now referred to as *early and intensive behavioral intervention*) involved 40 hours per week of educational efforts to reduce repetitive behaviors, teach the children to speak in words, increase compliance on tasks and imitate adults, and establish appropriate toy play. In the study, Lovaas suggested that almost half of the children "recovered" from their ASD, meaning that several years later teachers could not tell them apart from their students without ASD. Although criticized on methodological grounds, that study led the way for a growing research base supporting the value of early and intensive intervention for some children with ASD (Peters-Scheffer et al., 2011; Reichow & Wolery, 2009; Warren et al., 2011).

Several reviews of successful early intervention programs suggest a number of common features in each program:

- comprehensive curriculum focusing on imitation, language, toy play, social interaction, motor, and adaptive behavior;
- sensitivity to developmental sequence;
- supportive, empirically validated teaching strategies (applied behavior analysis);
- behavioral strategies for reducing interfering behaviors;
- involvement of parents;
- gradual transition to more naturalistic environments;
- highly trained staff;
- supervisory and review mechanisms;
- intensive delivery of treatment (25 hours per week for at least 2 years); and
- initiation by age 2–4 years (G. Dawson & Osterling, 1997; G. Green, Brennan, & Fein, 2002; National Research Council, 2001).

Approximately 50% of young children with ASD make impressive gains in IQ scores, adaptive behavior, and social communication skills when programs include these elements.

Some of these programs specifically target joint attention and play skills, the absence of which are some of the earliest signs of problematic social development (Bruinsma, Koegel, & Koegel, 2004; Whalen & Schreibman, 2003). Targeting these skills in the early years is potentially important for helping the child develop more sophisticated social repertoires (Mundy & Neal, 2000; Poon, Watson, Baranek, & Poe, 2012). A growing research base suggests that these skills can be facilitated among very young children with ASD (Lawton & Kasari, 2012; Wong & Kasari, 2012), and preliminary follow-up data suggest that this approach may facilitate later development of language (Kasari, Gulsrud, Freeman, Paparella, & Hellemann, 2012).

Researchers are now examining the characteristics of children that may predict the best outcomes (e.g., language ability, IQ score). In addition, some exciting research suggests that intensive early behavioral intervention may normalize the functioning of the developing brain in these children compared with children with ASD who do not receive the treatment (G. Dawson et al., 2012; Voos et al., 2013). Overall, the treatment progress seems to greatly improve for some children if intensive behavioral intervention is implemented early in life and with fidelity.

INTERVENTION FOR ASPERGER'S TYPE ASD

Individuals with Asperger's type ASD by definition do not have the cognitive delays often found in persons with Kanner's type, and with support they can do well academically. However, their social difficulties and common comorbid problems (e.g., attention-deficit/hyperactivity disorder, anxiety) complicate their interactions with peers and teachers and can lead to disruptive behavior problems. A number of programs exist to assist school-age children with Asperger's type ASD improve skills such as appropriate social interaction, problem-solving, self-control, recognizing emotions in others, expanding their often narrow range of interests, and improving their understanding of nonliteral idioms (Karkhaneh et al., 2010; Koning, Magill-Evans, Volden, & Dick, 2011; Laugeson, Frankel, Gantman, Dillon, & Mogil, 2012; Rao, Beidel, & Murray, 2008).

One randomized clinical trial that targeted social skills in this population is illustrative of a comprehensive package used to improve these abilities in students with Asperger's type ASD (Thomeer et al., 2012). This program used a 5-week summer camp as a backdrop for intensive work on a variety of social skills including social interactions, face–emotion recognition, interest expansion, and interpretation of nonliteral language. Seventeen children ranging in age from 7 to 12 years were randomly assigned to the treatment condition in groups with one staff member for every two children. Five 70-minute treatment sessions were conducted each day, 5 days per week. The sessions focused on a target skill and adapted the social skills curriculum called *Skillstreaming* (A. P. Goldstein & McGinnis, 1997). They found significant improvements in measures of knowledge of target social skills and understanding of idioms. On the other hand, there was not a significant improvement in facial–emotion recognition (Thomeer et al., 2012). Other programs specifically teach children how to make and maintain quality friendships (e.g., Program for the Evaluation and Enrichment of Relational Skills; Laugeson et al., 2012; Laugeson, Frankel, Mogil, & Dillon, 2009).

Although the techniques used to teach social skills to individuals with ASD having average and above cognitive abilities can be successful in improving their abilities to interact with others, it is important to remember their difficulties with empathy and "mind reading." Although they may be able to learn specific skills (e.g., how to approach a stranger and ask for assistance, how close to stand to someone, how to make appropriate eye contact), their abilities to feel and anticipate the emotions of others remain limited. This difficulty clearly puts them at a distinct disadvantage when trying to read others' expressions and body language. Teaching social skills is difficult enough even among those without ASD. The addition of the difficulty in reciprocal social exchange adds an additional level of challenge.

ADDRESSING SPECIAL NEEDS
IN INDIVIDUALS WITH ASD

A number of concerns pose additional challenges for individuals with ASD, their families, and their educators and employers: bullying, obsessiveness that resembles stalking, and the misperception that people with

Asperger's type ASD are more likely to be violent because of their tendency to be loners. Each of these issues is briefly described.

Bullying

Estimates of bullying of all students worldwide suggest that between 5% and 38% of girls and 6% to 41% of boys are bullied each year (Due et al., 2005). Unfortunately, the risk of being bullied increases significantly among those with ASD (Van Roekel, Scholte, & Didden, 2010). It appears that the social perception difficulties and unusual behaviors displayed by children and youth with ASD put them at higher risk of being victimized by other students. Students with Asperger's type ASD, for example, will often not be aware that another student is ridiculing them (e.g., Being told "You're so funny!" in a sarcastic tone of voice). The literal interpretation of language can lead to misperceptions about social situations. In addition, their unusual interests may make them stand out if they are not age appropriate (e.g., bringing a backpack to high school that has cartoon characters on it). Comorbid anxiety may make them appear vulnerable and may make them less likely to be able to stand up for themselves (Cappadocia, Weiss, & Pepler, 2012). Unusual responses to sensory stimulation (e.g., yelling out because of loud noise in a school cafeteria) can make them appear strange to other students (Humphrey & Symes, 2010). Having poor social skills and few friends denies them the group protection provided by peers. The concerns about bullying are increasing given the movement of these students into more inclusive settings. In addition, maternal reports of a child's suicidal ideation and attempts at suicide are significantly increased when they have experienced teasing or bullying (Mayes, Gorman, Hillwig-Garcia, & Syed, 2013).

Several approaches can help to reduce the risk of bullying in this population. At the individual level, the social skills training described previously can be geared to important social situations in school. For example, the group from UCLA conducting research on the Program for the Evaluation and Enrichment of Relational Skills curriculum included parents in sessions on how to assist their children with ASD with important social skills such as conversation; peer entry and exiting; developing friendship networks; good sportsmanship; good host behavior during get-togethers; changing bad reputations; and handling teasing, bullying, and arguments (Laugeson et al., 2009). Although programs such as these often report improvements in some social skills (Ozonoff & Miller, 1995), there are as yet no evidence-based individualized programs that document significant reductions in bullying in this population.

Stalking

Some of the social skills problems exhibited by individuals with ASD of the Asperger's type can not only cause them to be victims of teasing and bullying but, ironically, can also lead to situations that others can perceive as threatening (Stokes & Newton, 2004; Stokes, Newton, & Kaur, 2007). Jacob's mother, for example, described a situation that occurred when he was in high school and had become fixated on a particular girl in one of his classes. Jacob would follow her down the hall between classes and often show up at her house after school. Eventually the young woman complained to the school, and Jacob had to be counseled to stay away from her. Intervention research for stalking is in its infancy but parallels that of other challenging behaviors (e.g., assessing the function of stalking and teaching appropriate and replacement behaviors; Post, Haymes, Storey, Loughrey, & Campbell, 2012). The skills needed to reduce or prevent stalking include understanding the vocabulary for intimacy, distinguishing between acquaintances and friends, and understanding social rules and norms for approaching individuals.

Violence Among Persons With Asperger's Type ASD

Persons with Asperger's type ASD can sometimes become upset and lash out at others, especially if their desire for order is upset. However, rarely is this type of violent behavior premeditated (Gunasekaran & Chaplin, 2012). This concern became national news in December 2012 when a young man who was purported to have a diagnosis of Asperger's

Clinical Concerns: The Placebo Effect

People in a treatment group often expect to get better. When behavior changes as a result of a person's expectation of change rather than as a result of any intervention by a clinician, the phenomenon is known as a *placebo effect* (Durand & Barlow, 2010). In the case of ASD, especially among those with Kanner's type, it is unlikely that the individual will have expectations about a treatment's effect that change behavior. However, one area of concern in the field of ASD is the frequently observed placebo effect among parents (Goin-Kochel, Mackintosh, & Myers, 2009; Sandler, 2005). In other words, parents will sometimes report more significant positive behavior change in their child with ASD than is found by more objective measures.

Parents are hungry for help with the challenges faced by their children and often "shop around" for various tested and untested treatments. In fact, parents frequently report using multiple interventions for their child simultaneously, such as different diets or changes in programs for social communication skills along with changes in handling behavioral problems (Goin-Kochel, Myers, & Mackintosh, 2007; V. A. Green et al., 2006). Their hope for change and the often variable nature of symptoms of ASD (e.g., some days being better than others) may contribute to their seeing improvements in their child when none exist. In one large sample survey, most parents reported that every intervention tried with their child had a positive impact, even though the objective evidence for change with some of these treatments remains questionable (Goin-Kochel et al., 2009).

Although placebo effects observed in the treated individual can be a positive and important component of treatment (e.g., feeling less anxious or depressed due to expectation of a treatment's effect), seeing nondurable change in a child can lead parents to continue to use ineffective treatments, a costly choice in both price and effort. There are a number of important clinical implications for this placebo phenomenon for parents of children with ASD.

disorder stormed into Sandy Hook elementary school and killed 20 students and six school personnel. When this type of violence occurs by someone with an ASD diagnosis, evidence typically points to the presence of coexisting psychiatric disorders, such as major depression, obsessive–compulsive disorder, or various sexual disorders (Newman & Ghaziuddin, 2008). In fact, those with ASD are far more likely to be the victims of violence than the ones to commit such crimes (Hughes et al., 2012).

Clinicians should advise parents to make just one major change in their child's treatment at a time and to provide more objective methods for assessing improvement (e.g., a checklist of the number of words spoken each day). Preemptively warning parents about this phenomenon may also help them to become more effective participants in their child's treatments. Although parents can be an invaluable source of information about their child's behavior, care is needed when using parental report as the sole source of information about the effectiveness of interventions.

SUMMARY

Intervention is much more likely to be effective among those with Kanner's type ASD if it is delivered between the ages 2 and 4 and with appropriate fidelity and intensity (25 hours per week for at least 2 years). Some children who receive this type of early intervention show significant improvements, including perhaps permanent positive changes in the way their social brain functions. Treatment for those with Asperger's type ASD focuses on their social skills difficulties that stem from limitations in "reading the minds" of others and feeling empathy. Research suggests that many skills can be taught to help improve their chances of entering the social world of others, although there is not yet evidence for direct changes in theory of mind or the ability to empathize.

7

Addressing the Needs of Family Members

It is well-documented that parenting a child with autism spectrum dis-order (ASD) results in a great deal of stress (Abbeduto et al., 2004; Estes et al., 2009; Hoffman, Sweeney, Hodge, Lopez-Wagner, & Looney, 2009; Rao & Beidel, 2009). For example, Rao and Beidel (2009) studied reports of stress by parents of children with Asperger's type ASD and parents of matched control children. They found that parents of children with ASD experience significantly more parenting stress than parents of children with no psychological disorder and that the higher intellectual function-ing in children with ASD did not compensate for the stress associated with parenting children with ASD. In another example, Meirsschaut, Roeyers, and Warreyn (2010) studied the stress of mothers comparing their per-ceptions of their child with ASD with those of their typically developing child and found strong associations between mothers' symptoms of stress and depression and their parenting cognitions.

http://dx.doi.org/10.1037/14283-006
Autism Spectrum Disorder: A Clinical Guide for General Practitioners, by V. M. Durand

Although a variety of factors influence levels of stress among parents of children with ASD (e.g., their social communicative problems, efforts to secure appropriate services), problem behavior is routinely observed to be highly correlated with reports of elevated stress levels in these families (Hastings, 2002; Lecavalier, Leone, & Wiltz, 2006). A growing body of research demonstrates that when children with ASD engage in more problem behaviors, their parents are also likely to report more stress and other psychological symptoms such as anxiety and depression (Dumas, Wolf, Fisman, & Culligan, 1991; Eisenhower, Baker, & Blacher, 2005; Hastings, 2002; Hastings & Johnson, 2001; Lecavalier et al., 2006; Seltzer et al., 2010). In addition to self-reported levels of stress, biological markers have been found that support these verbal reports. Several important studies have begun to measure levels of cortisol (a hormonal marker for stress) among mothers of ASD children who display challenging behavior (Seltzer et al., 2010; L. E. Smith et al., 2010). The pattern of reaction to stress observed in these studies is striking; it is comparable in levels to findings in other groups experiencing chronic stress, including parents of children with cancer, combat soldiers, Holocaust survivors, and individuals suffering from posttraumatic stress disorder (Seltzer et al., 2010). As noted by L. E. Smith et al. (2010), "It is likely that these stressors accumulate over years of caregiving, potentially taking a cumulative toll on the wellbeing of mothers of individuals with ASD and further highlighting the need for appropriate family services" (p. 177). This is extremely important for clinicians who may have clients who present to them with the psychological consequences of such chronic stress (e.g., anxiety, depression). High levels of stress experienced by parents of children with ASD result in increases in immune system-related illnesses (Lovell, Moss, & Wetherell, 2012).

There is increasing recognition that parental attributional style significantly contributes to the stress of these families and ultimately to their ability to have a meaningful and happy home life (Solish & Perry, 2008; Whittingham, Sofronoff, Sheffield, & Sanders, 2009). *Parental attributions* are studied under a variety of labels but generally refer to parental perceptions about their child's ability to make behavioral improvements (*child efficacy*) as well as how parents view themselves and their role in parenting (*self-efficacy*). Research on the influence of child efficacy on parent training is limited in the field of ASD. In one exception, researchers found that participation in a parent training program (Stepping Stones Triple P) resulted in parents being less likely to believe that their child's problem behavior was caused by intrinsic factors and more likely to be capable of change in the future (Whittingham et al., 2009). These changes in attributional styles resulted in improved parental parenting practices (e.g., less overreactivity to problems). Parental attributions of their child's behavior may be important when assessing potential for successful intervention (Dale, Andrew, & Fiona, 2006).

Self-efficacy—parents' perceptions of their own ability to change their child's behaviors—has received more attention through the years (Hastings & Brown, 2002; Morrissey-Kane & Prinz, 1999). Substantial evidence suggests that parental self-efficacy influences child behavior both directly and indirectly (Jones & Prinz, 2005). For example, one study examined predictors of parental involvement in early intensive behavioral intervention (EIBI) with children with ASD. Parents and therapists completed a series of questionnaires aimed at seeing how parent self-efficacy, knowledge of autism, and belief in EIBI as an effective intervention predicted involvement in the program (Solish & Perry, 2008). Self-efficacy accounted for almost half of the variance related to who would or who would not participate—suggesting that feeling capable of implementing behavioral procedures is an important prerequisite to success.

Improving challenging behavior in children with ASD is one of the major priorities in the effort to improve the academic and social achievement of these children. Fortunately, our knowledge of the origins of these behaviors has increased over the past several decades along with our ability to respond to these behaviors in a positive, constructive way (e.g., Durand, 1990; Fox, Vaughn, Wyatte, & Dunlap, 2002). Behavioral parent training is typically used to assist parents with their children at home. This approach uses the principles of applied behavior analysis to help families develop the skills they need to support and manage their children's behavior (Durand, Hieneman, Clarke, Wang, & Rinaldi, 2013; Patterson, Smith, & Mirenda, 2012; Schultz, Schmidt, & Stichter, 2011). In general, behavioral parent training has been demonstrated to be effective, but effectiveness varies with the stressors being experienced by the family, the specific features of the intervention protocols, and the adjunctive supports being provided to the family (Aman et al., 2009; Drew et al., 2002; Durand et al., 2013; C. R. Johnson et al., 2007; Ozonoff & Cathcart, 1998). Clinicians require extensive training in order to provide this type of intervention for families; families should be referred to appropriate services to receive this type of assistance at home.

Some families are quite successful in taking on the two important roles of parent and advocate. As someone who has worked in the field for many years, I have seen those parents who make the transition from advocating just for their child to "taking on the system" in order to make services better for others as well. A qualitative study from Great Britain supports these impressions (Ryan & Cole, 2009). The researchers interviewed parents to get their perceptions of their roles as parents and found that whereas some parents were overwhelmed with the experience, others reported that the new challenges posed by their child actually had positive effects, such as making them feel better about themselves. Other parents ("*Über* parents") became autism activists. The study authors noted that the parents would not characterize themselves as "activists," perhaps because of negative connotations of the word. However, they described their evolution from going after help for their own child to trying to improve help for other children. For example, one parent of an 8-year-old son noted:

> I have been in talks with the National Autistic Society to get a representative to come to the school at some point to talk to the teachers and I also want to get the parents involved as well. . . . But they have also asked me—they want to raise the profile of disability in the school—and they have asked me whether or not I would be willing to be involved in that and the different things that are going on and of course I'm like "Yep, definitely." (Ryan & Cole, 2009, p. 48)

Unfortunately, my colleagues and I have found that in our work with families of children with ASD, almost half report pessimistic views about their own parenting abilities and their child's ability to change.

These cognitions can resemble depressive attributional styles (Seligman, Abramson, Semmel, & Von Baeyer, 1979). In other words, in addition to feelings of insecurity as parents and doubting their child's ability to improve his or her behaviors, they attribute bad outcomes to internal, stable, and global causes (e.g., attributing bad behavior to ASD). They also attribute positive outcomes (e.g., improvements seen in their child) to external and unstable causes (e.g., being in a good phase) and not to their own parenting. Both of these views can interfere with successful intervention with their child as well as with daily life and proper parenting (Durand, 2011c).

SUPPORT GROUPS

Fortunately, the number of local and regional support groups for families who have a child with ASD is vast both in the United States and internationally. Parents usually can be directed to these groups by a simple computer search for "autism support groups" in their area. These groups can be invaluable for family members who need assistance for themselves and their child. For example, parents who have older children on the autism spectrum may be able to assist others about the educational system in their area and identify good people to contact for proper services. In fact, because of the complexities of the educational system, it is usually recommended that parents find an experienced advocate to assist them in navigating the many intricacies of this process. In addition, seemingly simple things such as finding a dentist who is experienced and willing to work on a child who might be a challenge can be a godsend for a parent. More formal assistance can also be found through these groups, including gathering information on services such as early intervention, respite, assistive technology, camps, and recreational options.

Although these types of support groups can be very helpful for many parents, others report that groups make them feel uneasy. Pessimistic parents often report that being among these more confident and active parents makes them feel worse about themselves. Some mothers, for example, are able not only to handle their difficult child but also to help others, stay up on the latest research in the area, and even raise money for ASD-related causes. The more pessimistic parents feel that they are even more inadequate since they struggle on a daily basis just to keep from falling apart. These parents may require more focused clinical support.

ADJUNCTIVE COGNITIVE BEHAVIOR THERAPY (OPTIMISTIC PARENTING)

Optimistic parenting is an approach designed to assist parents with their child's disruptive behaviors as well as how to deal with their own insecurities and stress. This involves combining instruction in behavioral parent training with specific cognitive behavior therapy (CBT) focused on parenting cognitions that may interfere with success (Durand, 2011c). Because most current parent training programs do not address attitudinal obstacles or the stress, anxiety, or depression faced by these families, clinicians trained in CBT can be an important source of additional assistance. Clinicians can support these parents by assisting them with thoughts and beliefs that may interfere with their work with their child. The process begins with an assessment of parental beliefs about their child and themselves. Parents of children with ASD have specific areas of concern (see Durand, 2011c), and clinicians can start by exploring thoughts that may interfere with parenting and contribute to parental stress. Exhibit 7.1 lists some of the more common themes and examples of self-statements. Alternate positive thoughts can be encouraged in therapy.

In the case of Maria (see Chapter 1), her mother was experiencing significant difficulties with depression and anxiety. When Selena first contacted us about her daughter's behavior problems, we discussed how she viewed herself as a mother and how she viewed Maria's behaviors. She told us that she often felt inadequate as a parent in part because work demands prevented her from spending time with Maria. "I feel that I have no control over her. She cries and screams and I just don't know what to do." She was upset as she told us this and looked embarrassed. "And when we are out in public or at a relative's house I feel that people see me as a bad mother. They just don't understand that Maria has autism and that she can't control herself." You can see that in this brief interchange Selena

Exhibit 7.1

Common Themes Among Parents

1. How you see yourself as a parent (Self-efficacy)
   Parents have general thoughts about their inability to help their child. Feeling that things are "out of control" are common.

   Negative thoughts
   Theme: I cannot control my child.

   Alternate positive thoughts
   Theme: I am usually able to handle problem situations.

   Theme: I have doubts about my ability to help my child improve his/her behavior.

   Theme: I am capable of helping my child improve.

2. How you think others see you as a parent (Concern about others and self)
   This theme involves thoughts about being judged as a parent because of the child's unusual behaviors. This can cause parents to second-guess their parenting strategies.

   Negative thought
   Theme: When my child misbehaves, people see me as a bad parent.

   Alternate positive thought
   Theme: I believe I am a good parent.

3. How you think others view your child (Concern about others and child)
   Parents sometimes express anxiety about how other children or adults view their child. They are sometimes afraid that others will see their child as strange or unusual, and as a result they avoid taking their child into public spaces.

   Negative thought
   Theme: I think that other people judge my child when he/she is misbehaving.

   Alternate positive thought
   Theme: Most parents have times when their child misbehaves.

(continued)

Exhibit 7.1

Common Themes Among Parents (*Continued*)

4. How you see your child's ability control his/her behavior
   (Child efficacy)
   Parents sometimes doubt whether their child can improve his
   or her behavior; they might believe that the behavior is due to
   the disorder or just have a general pessimistic belief about the
   prospect for improvement.

   Negative thoughts   *Alternate positive thought*
   Theme: My child is not capa-   Theme: My child is capable
   ble of behaving better.   of behaving better.

   Theme: My child's behavior
   is related to the disability.

5. How you view the problem situation (Pervasive)
   This aspect of the thoughts of some parents involves catastrophizing bad situations (e.g., tantrum in a store). This can lead
   avoiding certain situations (e.g., shopping) or anxious antici-
   pation of future problems.

   Negative thought   *Alternate positive thought*
   Theme: All of these situations Theme: This particular inci-
   are always a major problem.   dent was a problem.

6. How you view the future (Stable)
   The problems they are experiencing are viewed as permanent,
   often even when objective information suggests that the child
   is indeed improving.

   Negative thoughts   *Alternate positive thought*
   Theme: Things will never get   Theme: Things can and will
   better or will get worse.   get better.

   Theme: I will never have my
   own life.

Exhibit 7.1

Common Themes Among Parents

7. Who is responsible for a problem situation (Blame–child)
   This theme is especially prevalent among parents who have children on the less extreme end of the autism spectrum. There can be resentment that their child is being egocentric and selfish.

Negative thought	*Alternate positive thought*
Theme: My child is doing this on purpose.	Theme: My child is not intentionally being disruptive.

8. Who is responsible for a problem situation (Blame–others)
   Parents perseverate on how others treat their child and how that interferes with their own success at home. Conflicts arise with teachers, relatives, or former spouses through disagreements over discipline.

Negative thought	*Alternate positive thought*
Theme: If only others would follow my suggestions correctly, my child would be better behaved.	Theme: Everyone is doing their best under the circumstances.

9. Who is responsible for a problem situation (Blame–self)
   Many parents express feeling guilt about how their child behaves and look to their "mistakes" in the past and blame themselves.

Negative thought	*Alternate positive thought*
Theme: It is my fault that things are going wrong.	Theme: I am doing the best that I can under the circumstances.

(continued)

Exhibit 7.1

Common Themes Among Parents (*Continued*)

10. Who should be responsible for the problem situation (Self-concern) Some parents may resent their role as being in charge of their child's care and feel sorry for themselves.

Negative thought	*Alternate positive thought*
Theme: Why am I always the one who has to be responsible for these situations?	Theme: Everyone is doing the best they can under the circumstances.

---

touched on at least three of the themes described. First, she described feeling out of control. This is one of the more common experiences of parents of children with ASD. Unfortunately, it is also one of the more troubling perceptions because feeling helpless in important situations can lead to symptoms of depression and as a result parents just give up (e.g., giving in to a child's demand for ice cream at breakfast). It can also lead to anticipatory anxiety over impending problems (e.g., getting on the schoolbus or going to a doctor's appointment where their child acts out). Selena told us that she let Maria eat dinner on the floor in the living room because it was easier than fighting with her to sit at the dinner table. But giving in to her contributed to her feeling that she was a poor parent.

Selena also confided that she felt judged by others. "My brother tells me I should be stricter with her, but he just doesn't understand. I can tell he disapproves of how I handle her and this makes me not want to visit him and his family." In fact, Selena told us that she was becoming more isolated because going out with Maria in public was so difficult. So not only was she feeling that things were out of her control, but she was also separating herself from the outside world, both of which could contribute to her deepening depression.

Selena expressed the belief that Maria could not behave better because of her "autism." This belief that a child is not capable of behaving better because of a disorder is not unique to ASD, but it appears to be more common in the context of ASD, possibly because of the unusual nature of some of their behaviors (e.g., the restricted and repetitive behaviors). However, also contributing to this perception is the social difficulties of those with ASD. Those with ASD are not sensitive to social discipline and often lack the concern felt by others over disapproval by a parent or authority figure (e.g., teacher). This results in a failure of some of the more common parenting techniques, such as expressing disappointment (e.g., "You are making mommy very upset"), because social sanctions have minimal impact on those with ASD. This belief that the child is not capable of behaving better is particularly problematic because it can lead to multiple concessions on the part of parents (e.g., letting the child wear the same shirt every day, always taking the same route to the store, not going to other's homes), which literally and figuratively "traps" families in their homes (Durand, 2011c).

If a clinician is working with a parent who is impacted by child problems at home (e.g., a child with ASD who is particularly challenging), several approaches may be appropriate. Referral for appropriate treatment for the child may be necessary, but the clinician can complement behavioral parent training by encouraging more optimistic views of the child and the parent's own ability to make changes in the child's behavior (i.e., CBT focusing on the reported feelings of inadequacy as a parent or beliefs that the child cannot change). Results from a recent randomized clinical trial suggest that adding CBT to traditional behavioral parent training can enhance the outcomes for both child and parents (Durand et al., 2013). In other words, parents are more successful at helping their child behave better when they take a more optimistic approach to themselves and their child.

In Selena's case, my colleagues and I identified recurrent themes in the thoughts she was having about herself and her daughter and encouraged her to practice being aware of these thoughts, especially in difficult situations (e.g., during one of Maria's tantrums). We gave her a log and asked her to record each of Maria's major tantrums as well as her thoughts

---

Clinical Concerns: Role of the Family in Treatment

Current successful interventions for children, youth, and adults with ASD rely on collaboration with parents and other caregivers. Follow-up at home and in the community on efforts to improve the behaviors of these individuals is essential. There is no treatment that can "fix" a child's behavior problems without parental involvement. However, it is common for more pessimistic parents to look for such solutions. The feelings of helplessness and hopelessness can often focus parents' search for help on approaches that removes them from the challenging role of parenting these individuals. Some parents will explicitly ask, "Can't you just fix him?" Other parents go on endless searches for diets (e.g., gluten-free/casein-free diet), nutritional supplements, and sometimes even dangerous medical treatments (e.g., chelation therapy, which allegedly removes mercury from the body but which can lead to liver and kidney damage). Clinicians may need to explain that there are no quick fixes and that parents must be partners in treatment. Starting the discussion with how they are handling their difficult child and their own personal struggles can open the door to further discussions and create an alliance that can help parents cope with future challenges.

---

at the time (Durand & Hieneman, 2008b). A sample entry can be seen in Figure 7.1.

Getting this type of information took some practice on Selena's part, and we needed to help her gain some insight into these thoughts. At first she would just report the emotions she was experiencing, such as feeling upset, frustrated, or embarrassed. However, thoughts such as "My whole family is looking at me and thinking I'm a terrible parent" required some prompting to help her put them into words (e.g., "What about the situation made you feel embarrassed?" "What do you think your family thought about Maria's tantrum?"). After she verbalized the thought that

Situation What happened?	Thoughts What did you think or say to yourself when this happened?	Feelings What emotions did you experience and how did you react physically when this happened?	Consequences What happened as a result of your thoughts and feelings?
We were at my mother's house, and Maria started to run around grabbing things off the coffee table and bookcases.	*I thought, "My whole family is looking at me and thinking I'm a terrible parent."*	*I was embarrassed and started to have an anxiety attack.*	*We left the house immediately, and I didn't get to enjoy the day with my family.*

Figure 7.1

Sample thoughts log entry for Selena. From *Optimistic Parenting: Hope and Help for You and Your Challenging Child* (p. 296), by V. M. Durand, 2011, Baltimore, MD: Paul H. Brookes. Copyright 2011 by Paul H. Brooks. Adapted with permission.

others view her as a bad mother with no control over Maria, the therapist could follow up with her and show her that it wasn't the tantrum itself that was embarrassing but the implication that she was a bad mother. We had her practice this self-reflection so that she could see what her thoughts were and that some of these thoughts led to unwanted consequences (e.g., missing out on a fun day with her family).

When Selena was becoming comfortable identifying her interfering thoughts, we adapted and implemented techniques from Seligman's (1998) version of CBT (*learned optimism*) to help her with these interfering thoughts. First, we went through the disputation process to challenge the validity and usefulness of these thoughts. For example, Selena reported, "My whole family is looking at me and thinking I'm a terrible parent." We were able to point out that most of her family thought she was working very hard with Maria and doing her best as a parent given Maria's difficulties. We also discussed how thinking that all of these visits will go poorly (a) made her feel badly about herself as a mother and (b) made her anxious and panicky when anticipating another similar outing. These thoughts actually interfered with her ability to put limits on Maria, which was counterproductive. In other words, these interfering thoughts were not completely true, and they were not useful to her as a parent. We added practice in disputation with Selena to her daily thought log (see the sample entry in Figure 7.2).

We needed to specifically target Selena's style of catastrophizing situations and have her catch herself when this happened. Over time she became better at verbalizing these thoughts (e.g., "Shopping with Maria is always a disaster") and reframing them in words that were more accurate (e.g., "Well, it's not all shopping trips. She does well when the trips are short and she isn't tired"). She became much better at refuting these thoughts by herself.

Situation What happened?	Thoughts What did you think or say to yourself when this happened?	Feelings What emotions did you experience and how did you react physically when this happened?	Consequences What happened as a result of your thoughts and feelings?	Disputation Were your thoughts accurate and useful?
We were rushing to get to the preschool on time, and I didn't let Maria line up her toys in her bedroom the way she likes. She started to scream and yell, but we were late so I had to drive her to the program screaming all the way.	*I thought, "This will never end. She will always have these problems." I also questioned whether or not this will ever get better and will I ever have time just for myself.*	*I was anxious not to be late. I felt angry at her for giving me such a hard time and felt sorry for myself.*	*My impatience led to my not taking the 60 seconds necessary to let her line up her toys, which resulted in her tantrum.*	*She is getting better at these things—not taking quite so long to get ready. I guess my thoughts weren't useful because dealing with her tantrum took more time than if I had allowed her to line up the toys.*

Figure 7.2

Sample thoughts log entry with disputation practice. From *Optimistic Parenting: Hope and Help for You and Your Challenging Child* (p. 296), by V. M. Durand, 2011, Baltimore, MD: Paul H. Brookes. Copyright 2011 by Paul H. Brooks. Adapted with permission.

An additional technique used in optimistic parenting is *substitution*. This exercise teaches parents to practice new thoughts that make them feel more optimistic and confident about their own abilities and their child's progress. Figure 7.3 illustrates one example from our work with Selena.

As can be seen from Selena's journal entry, she was beginning to substitute her thoughts about Maria being out of control and her own insecurities as a parent with more productive thoughts. Note too that Selena's religious faith was important to her, so we encouraged her to view these situations from that point of view. She told us that when she discussed her struggles with Maria in conversations with her priest, he pointed out that God specially chose her and her husband to be Maria's parents and that He did that because He knew Maria would be in good hands. This thought made Selena feel better about herself, and we encouraged her to practice substituting these types of thoughts for less productive ones.

Finally, we taught Selena to practice *distraction* when Maria's behavior put her in a particularly bad mood. The idea for distraction as a

Situation What happened?	Thoughts What did you think or say to yourself when this happened?	Feelings What emotions did you experience and how did you react physically when this happened?	Substitution What is a more positive way to think about this?
Maria sat down at the dinner table. Before I could get the food to the table, she climbed out of her chair and sat on the floor screaming.	*She is so out of control. I really am at my limit, and I don't know what to do. I should be better at handling this, but I'm not.*	*I was starting to feel anger at her, but then I felt so defeated and guilty that if I were better at dealing with her, she would behave better.*	*I am a good mother and I am trying to help her. God does not give us challenges that we cannot handle. I am getting this training with your help, and we will get this under control.*

Figure 7.3

Sample thoughts log entry with substitution practice. From *Optimistic Parenting: Hope and Help for You and Your Challenging Child* (p. 296), by V. M. Durand, 2011, Baltimore, MD: Paul H. Brookes. Copyright 2011 by Paul H. Brooks. Adapted with permission.

technique was to have Selena put a more positive spin on problem situations. We work on having parents become aware of a problem thought and then refocus their attention on something else. One example can be seen in Figure 7.4.

Selena's ability to make light of some of the difficulties with her daughter played an important role in her ability to work better with Maria at home. First, finding something fun to do along with necessary chores (e.g., brushing her teeth, getting dressed) made it more pleasant for Maria and helped to contribute to a more pleasant and successful experience. At the same time, it helped Selena deal with the situation more successfully. Clinicians may recognize some similarities between this goal and the goals of acceptance and commitment therapy (Hayes, Strosahl, & Wilson, 1999), which is designed to help individuals reframe difficult situations and learn how to be mindful of these struggles and not avoid them. One mechanism for why this might be beneficial is that it helps the individual to confront

Situation What happened (success or difficulty)?	Thoughts What did you think or say to yourself when this happened?	Feelings What emotions did you experience and how did you react physically when this happened?	Distraction What did you do to shift your attention?
I got Maria into the bathroom to wash up. When I took out the toothbrush and toothpaste, she started crying and fell on the floor.	I thought, "Why is she doing this to me? I'm tired from working all day, and I don't need this. Why didn't my husband brush her teeth earlier? I guess this is my 'job' and no one else can do it."	I felt upset at Maria and angry with my husband. I felt the muscles in my neck tighten up.	I started to sing a song with Maria about brushing her teeth. We saw this in a movie (Pee-wee's Big Adventure). This made us both smile and refocused me on a fun thing.

Figure 7.4

Sample thoughts log entry with distraction practice. From *Optimistic Parenting: Hope and Help for You and Your Challenging Child* (p. 296), by V. M. Durand, 2011, Baltimore, MD: Paul H. Brookes. Copyright 2011 by Paul H. Brooks. Adapted with permission.

negative thoughts and events, thereby reducing anxiety with continued exposure. In Selena's case we wanted her to become more comfortable with Maria's tantrums and not see them as calamitous. By not avoiding these conflicts but instead facing them, Selena became less anxious when they occurred, which in turn allowed her to be more confident with any disciplinary plans we recommended that she use with her daughter.

An additional technique we use with many parents is adapted from mindfulness therapy (Kabat-Zinn, 1995). Mindfulness therapy often uses meditation exercises to help people practice being aware of internal (e.g., breathing, thoughts) and external (e.g., noises) experiences occurring at the present time; it has been shown to be helpful with disorders such as anxiety and depression (Baer, 2003; Segal, Williams, & Teasdale, 2012). In our work we encourage mindfulness with parents when they are interacting with their children. Although they are all too aware of their child's behavior during a tantrum, their thoughts often drift away during the good times. For example, one mother with whom we worked reported that her son had a good bath that week (a rarity), but when we asked if she praised him, she reluctantly admitted she had not. When we pressed for more details, she said that she was too busy that day and her thoughts revolved around why she always had to give him a bath and why her husband did not help. For decades clinicians have been trying to get parents to praise their child when they behave well ("Catch them being good"), but often with limited success. We find that parents do not focus on good behavior because when their child is behaving well, their thoughts drift to chores and other obligations (e.g., the next task to tackle) or they ruminate on negative thoughts. The mother who gave her son a bath told us that while he was having a good bath she was wondering to herself why baths are such a problem for him because he liked to swim in the pool. This is consistent with a depressive attributional style, believing problems such as his bath-time disruptions are likely to continue to be a problem. Mindfulness is one technique that can help parents see that their child's behavior may not always be a problem; it can change over time (Durand & Hieneman, 2008a).

My colleagues and I just completed a series of major studies of a group of pessimistic parents, those who have considerable difficulty helping their child with ASD. In one group, we taught parents how to help their child behave better at home and out in the community. In the second group, we taught the same parenting skills but added optimism training. We taught them how to be aware of their interfering thoughts (e.g., "He's screaming at the store and I know other people think I'm a bad mother") and how to interrupt or replace them (e.g., "He's screaming but I know how to handle it and I have a plan"). We found that optimistic parenting helped them improve their child's behavior (Durand et al., 2013). These parents were better able to get their children to engage in sometimes unpleasant tasks and routines, and this helped the optimistic parents feel less stress and more in control (Durand, 2011a). The group that received behavioral parent training only continued to avoid difficulties with their child, which often led to more difficult problems as the child grew older (the *concession process*). Other research is finding that this type of concession in parents of children with ASD can lead to avoiding anxiety-producing situations for the child, which prevents exposure and reduced anxiety (Reaven & Hepburn, 2006). Other studies find that many parents of children with ASD are overprotective at bedtime (e.g., sleeping in their child's bed until he or she falls asleep), and this can contribute to maintaining sleep problems (Chou et al., 2012). All of this helps explain why some parents become trapped in their homes and develop feelings of helplessness.

THE SPECIAL CASE OF SIBLINGS

Siblings can help one another navigate a complex social world. Although not all siblings get along during all developmental periods, they can be good role models for important social interchanges (e.g., learning to share, regulating emotions). Some of the research involving typically developing siblings has been focused on using them as intervention agents in the family. To increase the opportunities for a child with ASD to have successful social interactions with other children outside of the school setting, researchers have evaluated how brothers or sisters could help extend the occasions for learning and practicing socially related behaviors. For example, one group taught older brothers and sisters of four children with

ASD how to encourage their younger siblings to use imitation ("Do what I do") during playtime using a procedure labeled *reciprocal imitation training* (Walton & Ingersoll, 2012). They found that the siblings could carry out these procedures, which resulted in three of the four children with ASD improving their ability to imitate and all four improving their skills in joint attention, an important early social skill. Other studies target behaviors such as play and other social skills (e.g., Castorina & Negri, 2011; Ferraioli & Harris, 2011; Oppenheim-Leaf, Leaf, Dozier, Sheldon, & Sherman, 2012).

However, being the brother or sister of a child with ASD brings other challenges. Jacob's younger sister, Bonnie, for example, described how in middle school she was embarrassed by her brother. She said he was a "know it all" who often corrected his peers and her friends and would also point things out about people that made them upset (e.g., saying to a classmate, "You have ugly braces on your teeth"). Bonnie told us that she never brought friends home and that she avoided Jacob when she was with her friends in the playground at school. The experiences of siblings can be quite disparate. Although some studies find that the experience of being a sibling of a child with ASD can sometimes be negative (e.g., Kaminsky & Dewey, 2001), other studies find siblings to be well-adjusted and to experience positive aspects of growing up with a sibling with ASD (Hastings, 2007; Kaminsky & Dewey, 2002; Pilowsky, Yirmiya, Doppelt, Gross-Tsur, & Shalev, 2004).

Several models can be used to work with individuals facing the challenges posed by a brother or sister with ASD, although there is relatively little research on the most effective ways of supporting siblings. Obviously, encouraging parents to have frank conversations with their typically developing child about their experiences can be helpful and sometimes enlightening (Tsao, Davenport, & Schmiege, 2012). One of the most popular group approaches is the Sibshops program, a workshop-like series of activities with a group of young children who all have brothers or sisters with ASD (Meyer & Vadasy, 1994). Activities are designed to be fun and have the following goals: to meet other siblings, to discuss the joys and challenges of having a sibling with ASD, to learn about their siblings special needs, and to discuss strategies for dealing with difficulties (e.g., telling their parents that they sometimes feel neglected or that they are sometimes embarrassed by their sibling's behaviors). These types of programs help raise awareness of siblings' special needs and provide the support that comes with knowing that others face similar experiences, but there is relatively little empirical data on the types of children who might benefit and the outcomes that might be expected (Conway & Meyer, 2008; Zona, Christodulu, & Durand, 2004).

SUMMARY

Family members of a person with ASD need support from many sources in order to handle the unique challenges posed by their child. There are now many organizations (e.g., the National Autism Society) that can provide appropriate referrals for a wide range of needs. It is also important that clinicians familiarize themselves with the needs of these individuals. Fortunately, clinicians trained in CBT can provide valuable assistance to these parents and caregivers that can not only improve their own well-being but also assist them with the parenting challenges they face. Siblings can be a source of assistance, but they must be monitored closely to assess how their experiences are affecting their own emotional and behavioral development.

Glossary

ACCEPTANCE AND COMMITMENT THERAPY   Behaviorally based therapeutic approach that strives to help individuals reframe difficult situations and learn how to be mindful of these struggles and not avoid them.

ADOPTION STUDIES   In genetics research, the study of first-degree relatives reared in different families and environments. If they share common characteristics, such as a disorder, the characteristics are likely to have a genetic component.

ALLELE   One member of a pair that represents a gene at a specific genetic locus on a chromosome.

AMYGDALA   Part of the brain's limbic system that regulates emotions and the ability to learn and control impulses.

ANTECEDENT-BASED INTERVENTION   Practice involving modification of environmental factors in settings that prompt engagement in interfering behavior so that the factor no longer elicits this behavior.

APPLIED BEHAVIOR ANALYSIS   A variety of techniques based on basic learning principles (e.g., operant conditioning) that are used to teach skills and help reduce behavior problems in persons with autism spectrum disorder.

ASPERGER'S DISORDER PERVASIVE DEVELOPMENTAL DISORDER (*DSM–IV–TR*)   Condition characterized by impairments in social relationships and restricted or unusual behaviors but without the language delays.

ASSOCIATION STUDIES   Research strategies for comparing genetic markers in groups of people with and without a particular disorder.

AUGMENTATIVE COMMUNICATION STRATEGIES   Pictures or computer aids to assist people with communication deficits so that they can communicate.

AUTISM PARTNERSHIPS MODEL   Comprehensive treatment model that uses discrete trial teaching methods and is based on applied behavior analysis (McEachin & Leaf, 1999).

AUTISTIC DISORDER (AUTISM) PERVASIVE DEVELOPMENTAL DISORDER (*DSM–IV–TR*)   Condition characterized by significant impairment in social interactions and communication and restricted patterns of behavior, interest, and activity.

BROADER AUTISM PHENOTYPE   Set of characteristics of family members of children with autism spectrum disorder that may differ from the general population.

CENTER FOR AUTISM AND RELATED DISORDERS (CARD) MODEL   Comprehensive treatment model that uses discrete trial teaching methods and is based on applied behavior analysis (Keenan, Henderson, Kerr, & Dillenburger, 2006).

CHILD EFFICACY   Perception of a child's ability to change. In behavioral parenting it refers to how optimistic a parent is about a child's ability to behave better and improve other behaviors.

CHILDHOOD DISINTEGRATIVE DISORDER PERVASIVE DEVELOPMENTAL DISORDER   (*DSM–IV–TR*) Disorder that involves severe regression in language, adaptive behavior, and motor skills after a 2- to 4-year period of typical development.

CHILDREN'S TODDLER PROGRAM   Comprehensive treatment model for young children based on applied behavior analysis, used in inclusive settings (Stahmer & Ingersoll, 2004).

COMPUTER-AIDED INSTRUCTION   Use of computers to teach academic skills and to promote communication and language development and skills.

COPY NUMBER VARIANTS   Mutations that either create extra copies of a gene on one chromosome or result in the deletion of a gene, which in turn results in mismatched genetic functioning and disruption in typical brain development.

DE NOVO MUTATIONS   Changes in genes that occur initially in one family member as a result of a mutation in a germ cell (egg or sperm) of one of the parents or in the fertilized egg.

DENVER MODEL   Comprehensive treatment model (also called Early Start Denver Model for young children) that uses naturalistic and child-directed activities and is based on developmental and relationship-based concepts (Rogers et al., 2006).

DETERMINISTIC   In genetics, genes that lead to nearly a 100% chance of developing the associated disorder. These are rare in the population.

DIFFERENTIAL REINFORCEMENT   Use of reinforcement for either appropriate behaviors or the absence of problem behavior (using praise or other rewards) while ignoring inappropriate behaviors. By reinforcing behaviors that are more functional or incompatible with the interfering behaviors, interfering behaviors will decrease.

DIR (DEVELOPMENTAL, INDIVIDUAL DIFFERENCE, RELATION-SHIP-BASED) MODEL   Comprehensive treatment model (also known as FLOORTIME) that uses naturalistic and child-directed activities and is based on developmental and relationship-based concepts (Greenspan & Wieder, 2006).

DISCRETE TRIAL TRAINING   One-to-one instructional approach for teaching new skills and behaviors explicitly using instruction, prompting, response, consequence, and inter-trial interval. This is appropriate for skills with a definite beginning and end that can be taught in small repeated steps.

DISCRIMINATION TRAINING   Arrangement of experiences in which the person learns to respond under certain conditions and not to respond under other conditions.

DISPUTATION   Confronting clients with their negative thoughts and discussing the validity of these thoughts and their value.

DISTRACTION   Practicing being aware of a problem thought and then working on refocusing attention on something else.

DOUGLASS MODEL   Comprehensive classroom-based treatment model that uses discrete trial and incidental teaching methods and is based on applied behavior analysis (Harris, Handleman, Gordon, Kristoff, & Fuentes, 1991).

EARLY START DENVER MODEL   See DENVER MODEL

EDEN MODEL   Comprehensive classroom-based treatment model that uses discrete trial teaching methods and is based on applied behavior analysis (Holmes, 1998).

EPIGENETICS   Process by which environmental factors (e.g., maternal stress, diet during pregnancy) can alter gene functioning without actually changing DNA.

EXTINCTION   Learning process in which a response maintained by reinforcement in operant conditioning or pairing in classical conditioning decreases when that reinforcement or pairing is removed; also the procedure of removing that reinforcement or pairing.

FLOORTIME   See DIR (DEVELOPMENTAL, INDIVIDUAL DIFFERENCE, RELATIONSHIP-BASED) MODEL

FRAGILE X SYNDROME   Pattern of abnormality caused by a defect in the X chromosome resulting in intellectual disability, learning problems, and unusual physical characteristics, often accompanied by symptoms of autism spectrum disorder.

FUNCTIONAL BEHAVIOR ASSESSMENT   A variety of techniques and strategies used to identify the purposes of specific behaviors (e.g., to gain attention from others, to escape from an unpleasant situation). This information is used to design interventions for challenging behavior (e.g., FUNCTIONAL COMMUNICATION TRAINING).

FUNCTIONAL COMMUNICATION TRAINING   Teaching of speech or nonspeech communication skills to replace undesired behavior. The new skills are useful to the person and are maintained because of the effects they have on others.

GENETIC MARKERS   Inherited characteristic for which the chromosomal location of the responsible gene is known.

GENOME-WIDE ASSOCIATION STUDIES   Studies that examine the association between a particular allele and a diagnosis or trait within a population.

HANEN MODEL   Comprehensive treatment model involving parents that uses naturalistic and child directed activities and is based on developmental and relationship-based concepts (McConachie, Randle, Hammal, & Le Couteur, 2005).

HIGASHI MODEL   Comprehensive treatment model (also called *daily life therapy*) that emphasizes physical exercise, emotional stability, and intellectual stimulation (Larkin & Gurry, 1998).

INCIDENTAL TEACHING   Process of arranging the natural environment to encourage student interest and the use of prompting techniques to encourage social communication in this setting.

JOINT ATTENTION   A social skill that involves making reciprocal eye contact back and forth between one person and another.

LANCASTER MODEL   Comprehensive classroom-based treatment model that uses discrete trial teaching methods and is based on applied behavior analysis (Bruey & Vorhis, 2006).

LEAP MODEL (LEARNING EXPERIENCES: AN ALTERNATIVE PROGRAM FOR PRESCHOOLERS AND PARENTS)   Comprehensive treatment model for young children that uses discrete trial and incidental teaching methods and is based on applied behavior analysis and used in inclusive settings (Hoyson, Jamieson, & Strain, 1984).

LOVAAS INSTITUTE MODEL   Comprehensive treatment model for young children that uses discrete trial teaching methods and is based on applied behavior analysis (Cohen, Amerine-Dickens, & Smith, 2006).

MANUAL SIGN LANGUAGE   Use of hand gestures (usually those prescribed by American Sign Language) to communicate basic information in the absence of speech.

MAY INSTITUTE MODEL   Comprehensive classroom-based treatment model that uses discrete trial teaching methods and is based on applied behavior analysis (Campbell et al., 1998).

MILIEU TEACHING   A package of behaviorally based strategies that are used in normally occurring daily routines to address communication objectives. These strategies include model, mand-model, time delay, and incidental teaching.

MINDFULNESS THERAPY   An approach to therapy that emphasizes the use of meditation exercises to help people practice being aware of internal and external experiences occurring at the present time. It has been shown to be helpful with disorders such as anxiety and depression.

NATURALISTIC INTERVENTION   Use of a learner's interests or natural environment as an opportunity to teach or encourage specific behaviors. This approach uses environmental arrangement, interaction techniques, and behavioral strategies.

OPTIMISTIC PARENTING   Combination of instruction in behavioral parent training and specific cognitive behavior therapy focused on parenting cognitions that may interfere with success.

OXIDATIVE STRESS   A disruption in the normal process by which cells rid themselves of harmful free radicals.

OXYTOCIN   A brain hormone that appears to be involved in social bonding.

PARENT IMPLEMENTED INTERVENTION   Intervention strategies that are implemented by parents to create learning opportunities to help their children acquire specific skills and/or reduce challenging behavior.

PEER-MEDIATED INSTRUCTION AND INTERVENTION   Practice in which peers are taught how to interact with and engage learners with autism spectrum disorder as a way to help them acquire new social and play skills. Social opportunities are increased through teacher-directed and learner-initiated activities.

PICTURE EXCHANGE COMMUNICATION SYSTEM (PECS)   Communication-training program developed to facilitate communication for nonverbal children that allows them to express their needs.

PIVOTAL RESPONSE TREATMENT MODEL (PRT)   Comprehensive treatment model that uses discrete trial and incidental teaching methods and is based on applied behavior analysis (R. Koegel & Koegel, 2006). The model focuses on four key pivotal behaviors: response to multiple cues, motivation, self-management, and self-initiation.

PLACEBO EFFECT   Behavior change resulting from the person's expectation of change rather than from the experimental manipulation itself. In the field of autism spectrum disorder, this can involve parental expectations of child behavior change.

PLEIOTROPY   A single gene that is controlling or influencing multiple phenotypic traits. These traits may be unrelated to one another.

POLYSOMNOGRAPHIC EVALUATION   Assessment of sleep disorders in which a client sleeping in the lab is monitored for heart, muscle, respiration, brain wave, and other functions.

PRINCETON CHILD DEVELOPMENT INSTITUTE (PCDI) MODEL   Comprehensive classroom-based treatment model that uses discrete trial teaching methods and is based on applied behavior analysis (Fenske, Zalenski, Krantz, & McClannahan, 1985).

PROBABILISTIC   Genes that contribute in small ways to increase the chance of developing the associated disorder.

PROMPTING   Use of physical, verbal, model, gestural, or visual cues to induce desired behavior.

PROSODY   The tone of voice one uses in speaking. This can be unusual (e.g., speaking too loud, using a high pitched voice) in some persons with autism spectrum disorder.

PURKINJE CELLS   Large neurons that are found in the cerebellum of the brain and are involved with controlling motor movement.

RECIPROCAL GENE–ENVIRONMENT MODEL   Hypothesis that people with a genetic predisposition for a disorder may also have a genetic tendency to create environmental risk factors that promote the disorder.

REINFORCEMENT   In operant conditioning, consequences for behavior that strengthen it or increase its frequency. Positive reinforcement involves the contingent delivery of a desired consequence. Negative reinforcement is the contingent escape from an aversive consequence. Unwanted behaviors may result from reinforcement of those behaviors or the failure to reinforce desired behaviors.

RESPONSE INTERRUPTION/REDIRECTION   Practice used to decrease interfering behaviors, predominantly those that are repetitive, stereotypical, and/or self-injurious. The learner is stopped from engaging in the interfering behavior and is prompted to engage in a more appropriate behavior.

RESPONSIVE TEACHING MODEL   Comprehensive treatment model involving parents that uses naturalistic and child-directed activities based on developmental and relationship-based concepts (Mahoney & Perales, 2005).

SELF-EFFICACY   How parents view their abilities and effectiveness in parenting their child with autism spectrum disorder.

SELF-MANAGEMENT   The ability of learners with autism spectrum disorder to monitor their own behavior and act appropriately in different settings.

SENSITIVITY   Average percentage of "true positives" for an assessment tool, or accurately identifying someone with a disorder.

SHAPING   In operant conditioning, the development of a new response by reinforcing successively more similar versions of that response. Both desirable and undesirable behaviors may be learned in this manner.

SOCIAL COMMUNICATION, EMOTIONAL REGULATION, TRANS-ACTIONAL SUPPORTS (SCERTS) MODEL   Comprehensive treatment model that uses naturalistic and child-directed activities is based on developmental and relationship-based concepts (Prizant, Wetherby, Rubin, Laurent, & Rydell, 2006).

SOCIAL NARRATIVES   Short descriptions indicating important cues and appropriate responses or behaviors in various social settings that help learners adopt specific social skills. They may include pictures or other visual aids, which guide learners toward appropriate behaviors and responses.

SOCIAL SKILLS GROUPS   Small groups designed to help learners with autism spectrum disorder interact with peers through instruction, role-playing or practice, and feedback.

SON RISE   Comprehensive treatment model that uses naturalistic and child-directed activities and is based on developmental and relationship-based concepts (B. Kaufman, 1981).

SPECIFICITY   Average percentage of "true negatives" for an assessment tool or correctly identifying that someone does not have a specific disorder.

SPECIFIERS   Language included in a *DSM–5* diagnosis to allow for more descriptive information such as the course of the disorder or its origins (e.g., "Associated with Known Medical Disorder or Genetic Condition").

SPEECH GENERATING DEVICES   Portable, electronic devices that produce synthetic or digital speech for users who have limited or no verbal speech.

STRUCTURED WORK SYSTEMS   Systematic and organized visual presentation of tasks, which helps learners independently practice skills they have mastered without adult directions or prompts.

SUBSTITUTION   Technique wherein clients are taught to replace a negative thought (e.g., "I am a bad parent") with a more positive and useful thought (e.g., "I work hard at being a better parent and things are getting better").

SUMMIT MODEL   Comprehensive classroom-based treatment model that uses discrete trial teaching methods and is based on applied behavior analysis (S. R. Anderson, Thomeer, & King, 2006).

SYNDROMIC AUTISM   Cases of autism that are secondary to another identifiable disorder (e.g., Rett syndrome, fragile X syndrome, tuberous sclerosis, Smith-Lemli-Opitz syndrome).

TASK ANALYSIS   Process of breaking a task down into smaller, more manageable steps and mastering them one at a time.

TEACCH MODEL (TREATMENT AND EDUCATION OF AUTISTIC AND RELATED COMMUNICATION-HANDICAPPED CHILDREN)   Comprehensive classroom-based treatment model that uses discrete trial teaching methods and is based on applied behavior analysis. There is a strong focus on structured teaching, such as visual schedules and work stations (Panerai, Ferrante, & Zingale, 2002).

THEORY OF MIND   Ability to interpret one's own intentions and emotions and those of others.

TIME DELAY   Delay provided between instruction and prompt, allowing time to initiate the response or behavior. This delay can be constant or progressive and is geared toward eventual fading use of prompts.

TRIAD SOCIAL SKILLS ASSESSMENT   Criterion-based, multi-informant tool that is used to assess the social behaviors of individuals with autism spectrum disorder.

VIDEO MODELING   Use of videos of other children or the target person engaging in behaviors, which allows for modeling and feedback to teach social communication skills.

VISUAL SUPPORTS   Visual tools that encourage task engagement, social interaction, and play skill development.

References

Abbeduto, L., Seltzer, M. M., Shattuck, P., Krauss, M. W., Osmond, G., & Murphy, M. M. (2004). Psychological well-being and coping in mothers of youths with autism, Down syndrome, or fragile X syndrome. *American Journal on Mental Retardation, 109,* 237–254. doi:10.1352/0895-8017(2004)109<237:PWACIM> 2.0.CO;2

Achenbach, T. M., & Edelbrock, C. S. (1991). *The Child Behavior Checklist.* Department of Psychiatry, University of Vermont, Burlington.

Addington, A. M., & Rapoport, J. L. (2012). Annual research review: Impact of advances in genetics in understanding developmental psychopathology. *Journal of Child Psychology and Psychiatry, 53,* 510–518. doi:10.1111/j.1469-7610.2011.02478.x

Ahearn, W. H., Castine, T., Nault, K., & Green, G. (2001). An assessment of food acceptance in children with autism or pervasive developmental disorder-not otherwise specified. *Journal of Autism and Developmental Disorders, 31,* 505–511. doi:10.1023/A:1012221026124

Allen, G., & Courchesne, E. (2003). Differential effects of developmental cerebellar abnormality on cognitive and motor functions in the cerebellum: An fMRI study of autism. *The American Journal of Psychiatry, 160,* 262–273. doi:10.1176/appi.ajp.160.2.262

Allen, J., DeMyer, M., Norton, J., Pontius, W., & Yang, G. (1971). Intellectuality in parents of psychotic, subnormal, and normal children. *Journal of Autism and Childhood Schizophrenia, 1,* 311–326. doi:10.1007/BF01557351

Al-Qabandi, M., Gorter, J. W., & Rosenbaum, P. (2011). Early autism detection: Are we ready for routine screening? *Pediatrics, 128,* e211–e217. doi:10.1542/peds.2010-1881

Aman, M. G., McDougle, C. J., Scahill, L. M., Handen, B., Arnold, L. E., Johnson, C., . . . Wagner, A. (2009). Medication and parent training in children with pervasive developmental disorders and serious behavior problems: Results from a randomized clinical trial. *Journal of the American Academy of Child & Adolescent Psychiatry, 48,* 1143–1154. doi:10.1097/CHI.0b013e3181bfd669

Aman, M. G., Tasse, M. J., Rojahn, J., & Hammer, D. (1996). The Nisonger CBRF: A child behavior rating form for children and adolescents with developmental disabilities. *Research in Developmental Disabilities, 17,* 41–57. doi:10.1016/0891-4222(95)00039-9

Amaral, D. G., Dawson, G., & Geschwind, D. (Eds.). (2011). *Autism spectrum disorders.* New York, NY: Oxford University Press. doi:10.1093/med/9780195371826.001.0001

American Academy of Pediatrics. (2007). *Identification and evaluation of children with autism spectrum disorders.* Retrieved from http://www.medicalhomeinfo.org/downloads/pdfs/AutismAlarm.pdf

American Psychiatric Association. (2000). *Diagnostic and statistical manual of mental disorders* (4th ed., Text Revision). Washington, DC: Author.

American Psychiatric Association. (2013). *Diagnostic and statistical manual of mental disorders* (5th ed.). Washington, DC: Author.

American Psychological Association. (2010). *Ethical principles of psychologists and codes of conduct.* Washington, DC: Author. Retrieved from http://www.apa.org/ethics/code/index.aspx

Anderson, D. K., Lord, C., Risi, S., DiLavore, P. S., Shulman, C., Thurm, A., . . . Pickles, A. (2007). Patterns of growth in verbal abilities among children with autism spectrum disorder. *Journal of Consulting and Clinical Psychology, 75,* 594–604. doi:10.1037/0022-006X.75.4.594

Anderson, S. R., Thomeer, M. L., & King, D. C. (2006). *Summit academy: Implementing a system-wide intervention.* Austin, TX: PRO-ED.

Armstrong, T. (2010). *Neurodiversity: Discovering the extraordinary gifts of autism, ADHD, dyslexia, and other brain differences.* Cambridge, MA: Da Capo Press.

Asperger, H. (1991). "Autistic psychopathy" in childhood. In U. Frith (Ed.), *Autism and Asperger syndrome* (pp. 37–92). Cambridge, England: Cambridge University Press. (Original work published 1944) doi:10.1017/CBO9780511526770.002

Atladóttir, H. Ó., Henriksen, T. B., Schendel, D. E., & Parner, E. T. (2012). Autism after infection, febrile episodes, and antibiotic use during pregnancy: An exploratory study. *Pediatrics, 130,* e1447–1454. doi:10.1542/peds.2012-1107

Autism and Developmental Disabilities Monitoring Network. (2007). Prevalence of autism spectrum disorders-autism and developmental disabilities monitoring network, 14 sites, United States, 2002. *Morbidity and Mortality Weekly Report. Surveillance Summaries, 56,* 12–28.

Baer, R. A. (2003). Mindfulness training as a clinical intervention: A conceptual and empirical review. *Clinical Psychology: Science and Practice, 10,* 125–143. doi:10.1093/clipsy.bpg015

Baio, J. (2012). Prevalence of autism spectrum disorders—Autism and Developmental Disabilities Monitoring Network, 14 Sites, United States, 2008. *Morbidity and Mortality Weekly Report. Surveillance Summaries, 61*(3), 1–19. Atlanta, GA: Centers for Disease Control and Prevention.

Barclay, N. L., & Gregory, A. M. (2013). Quantitative genetic research on sleep: A review of normal sleep, sleep disturbances and associated emotional, behavioural, and health-related difficulties. *Sleep Medicine Reviews, 17,* 29–40. doi:10.1016/j.smrv.2012.01.008

Barnes, K. E. (1982). *Preschool screening: The measurement and prediction of children at-risk.* Springfield, IL: Charles C Thomas.

Baron-Cohen, S. (1997). *Mindblindness: An essay on autism and theory of mind.* Cambridge, MA: MIT Press.

Baron-Cohen, S. (2009, November 9). The short life of a diagnosis. *The New York Times,* p. A35. Retrieved from http://www.nytimes.com/2009/11/10/opinion/10baron-cohen.html

Baron-Cohen, S., Tager-Flusberg, H. E., & Cohen, D. J. (2000). *Understanding other minds: Perspectives from developmental cognitive neuroscience.* New York, NY: Oxford University Press.

Baron-Cohen, S., Wheelwright, S., Cox, A., Baird, G., Charman, T., Swettenham, J., . . . Doehring, P. (2000). Early identification of autism by the Checklist for Autism in Toddlers (CHAT). *Journal of the Royal Society of Medicine, 93,* 521–525.

Bartak, L., & Rutter, M. (1974). The use of personal pronouns by autistic children. *Journal of Autism and Childhood Schizophrenia, 4,* 217–222. doi:10.1007/BF02115227

Beardon, L., & Worton, D. (2011). *Aspies on mental health: Speaking for ourselves.* London, England: Kingsley.

Begeer, S., Bernstein, D. M., van Wijhe, J., Scheeren, A. M., & Koot, H. (2012). A continuous false belief task reveals egocentric biases in children and adolescents with Autism Spectrum Disorders. *Autism, 16,* 357–366. doi:10.1177/1362361311434545

Begeer, S., Gevers, C., Clifford, P., Verhoeve, M., Kat, K., Hoddenbach, E., & Boer, F. (2011). Theory of Mind training in children with autism: A randomized controlled trial. *Journal of Autism and Developmental Disorders, 41,* 997–1006. doi:10.1007/s10803-010-1121-9

Behar, L., & Stringfield, S. (1974). *Preschool Behavior Questionnaire.* Durham, NC: LINC Press.

Bellini, S., & Akullian, J. (2007). A meta-analysis of video modeling and video self-modeling interventions for children and adolescents with autism spectrum disorders. *Exceptional Children, 73*(3), 264–287.

Berg, A. T., & Plioplys, S. (2012). Epilepsy and autism: Is there a special relationship? *Epilepsy & Behavior, 23,* 193–198. doi:10.1016/j.yebeh.2012.01.015

Berger, R. H., Miller, A. L., Seifer, R., Cares, S. R., & Lebourgeois, M. K. (2012). Acute sleep restriction effects on emotion responses in 30- to 36-month-old children. *Journal of Sleep Research, 21,* 235–246. doi:10.1111/j.1365-2869.2011.00962.x

Bettelheim, B. (1967). *The empty fortress: Infantile autism and the birth of the self.* New York, NY: Free Press.

Bhasin, T. K., & Schendel, D. (2007). Sociodemographic risk factors for autism in a U.S. metropolitan area. *Journal of Autism and Developmental Disorders, 37,* 667–677. doi:10.1007/s10803-006-0194-y

Billstedt, E., Gillberg, I. C., & Gillberg, C. (2007). Autism in adults: Symptom patterns and early childhood predictors: Use of the DISCO in a community sample followed from childhood. *Journal of Child Psychology and Psychiatry, 48,* 1102–1110. doi:10.1111/j.1469-7610.2007.01774.x

Bishop, J., Huether, C. A., Torfs, C., Lorey, F., & Deddens, J. (1997). Epidemiologic study of Down syndrome in a racially diverse California population, 1989–1991. *American Journal of Epidemiology, 145,* 134–147. doi:10.1093/oxfordjournals.aje.a009084

Blumberg, S. J., Bramlett, M. D., Kogan, M. D., Schieve, L. A., & Jones, J. R. (2013). Changes in prevalence of parent-reported autism spectrum disorder in school-aged U.S. children: 2007 to 2011–2012. *National Health Statistics Reports,* no. 65. Hyattsville, MD: National Center for Health Statistics.

Bolton, P. F., Carcani-Rathwell, I., Hutton, J., Goode, S., Howlin, P., & Rutter, M. (2011). Features and correlates of epilepsy in autism. *The British Journal of Psychiatry, 198,* 289–294. doi:10.1192/bjp.bp.109.07687

Bondy, A. S., & Frost, L. A. (1994). The picture exchange communication system. *Focus on Autism and Other Developmental Disabilities, 9*(3), 1–19. doi:10.1177/108835769400900301

Boyd, B. A., McDonough, S., & Bodfish, J. (2012). Evidence-based behavioral interventions for repetitive behaviors in autism. *Journal of Autism and Developmental Disorders, 42,* 1236–1248. doi:10.1007/s10803-011-1284-z

Boyd, B. A., Woodard, C. R., & Bodfish, J. W. (2013). Feasibility of exposure response prevention to treat repetitive behaviors of children with autism and an intellectual disability: A brief report. *Autism, 17,* 196–204. doi:10.1177/1362361311414066

Breece, E., Paciotti, B., Nordahl, C. W., Ozonoff, S., Van de Water, J. A., Rogers, S. J., . . . Ashwood, P. (2012). Myeloid dendritic cells frequencies are increased in children with autism spectrum disorder and associated with amygdala volume and repetitive behaviors. *Brain, Behavior, and Immunity.* Retrieved from http://www.sciencedirect.com/science/article/pii/S0889159112004680

Brownell, R. (2000). *Expressive one-word picture vocabulary test.* Novato, CA: Academic Therapy.

Bruey, C. T., & Vorhis, N. (2006). The Lancaster-Lebanon IU 13 autism support program. In J. Handleman & S. Harris (Eds.), *School-age programs for children with autism* (pp. 115–142). Austin, TX: PRO-ED.

Bruinsma, Y., Koegel, R. L., & Koegel, L. K. (2004). Joint attention and children with autism: A review of the literature. *Mental Retardation and Developmental Disabilities Research Reviews, 10,* 169–175. doi:10.1002/mrdd.20036

Bryson, S. E., Zwaigenbaum, L., McDermott, C., Rombough, V., & Brian, J. (2008). The Autism Observation Scale for Infants: Scale development and reliability data. *Journal of Autism and Developmental Disorders, 38,* 731–738. doi:10.1007/s10803-007-0440-y

Buggey, T. (2012). Video modeling applications for persons with autism. In P. A. Prelock & R. J. McCauley (Eds.), *Treatment of autism spectrum disorders: Evidence based-intervention strategies for communication and social interactions* (pp. 345–369). Baltimore, MD: Brookes.

Buie, T., Campbell, D. B., Fuchs, G. J., Furuta, G. T., Levy, J., VandeWater, J., . . . Winter, H. (2010). Evaluation, diagnosis, and treatment of gastrointestinal disorders in individuals with ASDs: A consensus report. *Pediatrics, 125*(Suppl. 1), S1–S18. doi:10.1542/peds.2009-1878C

Buie, T., Fuchs, G. J., Furuta, G. T., Kooros, K., Levy, J., Lewis, J. D., . . . Winter, H. (2010). Recommendations for evaluation and treatment of common gastrointestinal problems in children with ASDs. *Pediatrics, 125*(Suppl. 1), S19–S29. doi:10.1542/peds.2009-1878D

Butzer, B., & Konstantareas, M. M. (2003). Depression, temperament and their relationship to other characteristics in children with Asperger's disorder. *Journal on Developmental Disabilities, 10,* 67–72.

Caglayan, A. O. (2010). Genetic causes of syndromic and non-syndromic autism. *Developmental Medicine & Child Neurology, 52,* 130–138. doi:10.1111/j.1469-8749.2009.03523.x

Calzada, L. R., Pistrang, N., & Mandy, W. (2012). High-functioning autism and Asperger's disorder: Utility and meaning for families. *Journal of Autism and Developmental Disorders, 42,* 230–243. doi:10.1007/s10803-011-1238-5

Campbell, S., Cannon, B., Ellis, J. T., Lifter, K., Luiselli, J. K., Navalta, C. P., & Taras, M. (1998). The May Center for Early Childhood Education: Description of a continuum of services model for children with autism. *International Journal of Disability, Development and Education, 45,* 173–187. doi:10.1080/1034912980450204

Cappadocia, M. C., Weiss, J. A., & Pepler, D. (2012). Bullying experiences among children and youth with autism spectrum disorders. *Journal of Autism and Developmental Disorders, 42,* 266–277. doi:10.1007/s10803-011-1241-x

Carr, E. G. (1979). Teaching autistic children to use sign language: Some research issues. *Journal of Autism and Developmental Disorders, 9,* 345–359. doi:10.1007/BF01531444

Carr, E. G., Binkoff, J. A., Kologinsky, E., & Eddy, M. (1978). Acquisition of sign language by autistic children. I: Expressive labelling. *Journal of Applied Behavior Analysis, 11,* 489–501. doi:10.1901/jaba.1978.11-489

Carrasco, M., Volkmar, F. R., & Bloch, M. H. (2012). Pharmacologic treatment of repetitive behaviors in autism spectrum disorders: Evidence of publication bias. *Pediatrics, 129,* e1301–1310. doi:10.1542/peds.2011-3285

Castorina, L. L., & Negri, L. M. (2011). The inclusion of siblings in social skills training groups for boys with Asperger syndrome. *Journal of Autism and Developmental Disorders, 41,* 73–81. doi:10.1007/s10803-010-1023-x

Chalfant, A. M., Rapee, R., & Carroll, L. (2007). Treating anxiety disorders in children with high functioning autism spectrum disorders: A controlled trial. *Journal of Autism and Developmental Disorders, 37,* 1842–1857. doi:10.1007/s10803-006-0318-4

Charlop-Christy, M. H., Le, L., & Freeman, K. A. (2000). A comparison of video modeling with in vivo modeling for teaching children with autism. *Journal of Autism and Developmental Disorders, 30,* 537–552. doi:10.1023/A:1005635326276

Chauhan, A., & Chauhan, V. (2006). Oxidative stress in autism. *Pathophysiology, 13,* 171–181. doi:10.1016/j.pathophys.2006.05.007

Chervin, R. D., Hedger, K., Dillon, J. E., & Pituch, K. J. (2000). Pediatric sleep questionnaire (PSQ): Validity and reliability of scales for sleep-disordered breathing, snoring, sleepiness, and behavioral problems. *Sleep Medicine, 1*(1), 21–32. doi:10.1016/S1389-9457(99)00009-X

Chou, M.-C., Chou, W.-J., Chiang, H.-L., Wu, Y.-Y., Lee, J.-C., Wong, C.-C., & Gau, S. S.-F. (2012). Sleep problems among Taiwanese children with autism, their siblings and typically developing children. *Research in Autism Spectrum Disorders, 6*(2), 665–672. doi:10.1016/j.rasd.2011.09.010

Cohen, H., Amerine-Dickens, M., & Smith, T. (2006). Early intensive behavioral treatment: Replication of the UCLA Model in a community setting. *Journal of Developmental & Behavioral Pediatrics, 27,* S145–S155. doi:10.1097/00004703-200604002-00013

Committee on Bioethics, Committee on Genetics, and The American College of Medical Genetics and Genomics Social, Ethical, and Legal Issues Committee. (2013). Ethical and policy issues in genetic testing and screening of children. *Pediatrics, 131,* 620–622. doi:10.1542/peds.2012-3680

Conners, C. K. (2008). *Conners Comprehensive Behavior Rating Scales manual.* Toronto, Canada: Multi-Health Systems.

Constantino, J. N., & Gruber, C. P. (2002). *The Social Responsiveness Scale.* Los Angeles, CA: Western Psychological Services.

Conway, S., & Meyer, D. (2008). Developing support for siblings of young people with disabilities. *Support for Learning, 23,* 113–117. doi:10.1111/j.1467-9604.2008.00381.x

Council on Children With Disabilities, Section on Developmental Behavioral Pediatrics, Bright Futures Steering Committee, & Medical Home Initiatives for Children With Special Needs Project Advisory Committee (2006). Identifying infants and young children with developmental disorders in the medical home: An algorithm for developmental surveillance and screening. *Pediatrics, 118,* 405–420. doi:10.1542/peds.2006-1231

Courchesne, E., Webb, S. J., & Schumann, C. M. (2011). From toddlers to adults: The changing landscape of the brain in autism. In D. G. Amaral, G. Dawson, & D. Geschwind (Eds.), *Autism spectrum disorders* (pp. 611–631). New York, NY: Oxford University Press. doi:10.1093/med/9780195371826.003.0040

Couturier, J. L., Speechley, K. N., Steele, M., Norman, R., Stringer, B., & Nicolson, R. (2005). Parental perception of sleep problems in children of normal intelligence with pervasive developmental disorders: Prevalence, severity, and pattern. *Journal of the American Academy of Child & Adolescent Psychiatry, 44,* 815–822. doi:10.1097/01.chi.0000166377.22651.87

Cox, A., Rutter, M., Newman, S., & Bartak, L. (1975). A comparative study of infantile autism and specific developmental receptive language disorder: II. Parental characteristics. *The British Journal of Psychiatry, 126,* 146–159. doi:10.1192/bjp.126.2.146

Crimmins, D. B., Durand, V. M., Theurer-Kaufman, K., & Everett, J. (2001). *Autism program quality indicators: A self-review and quality improvement guide for schools and programs serving students with autism spectrum disorders.* Albany: New York State Department of Education.

Croen, L. A., Najjar, D. V., Fireman, B., & Grether, J. K. (2007). Maternal and paternal age and risk of autism spectrum disorders. *Archives of Pediatrics & Adolescent Medicine, 161,* 334–340. doi:10.1001/archpedi.161.4.334

Dale, E., Andrew, J., & Fiona, K. (2006). Mothers' attributions following their child's diagnosis of autistic spectrum disorder: Exploring links with maternal levels of stress, depression and expectations about their child's future. *Autism, 10,* 463–479. doi:10.1177/1362361306066600

Dawson, G. (2008). Early behavioral intervention, brain plasticity, and the prevention of autism spectrum disorder. *Development and Psychopathology, 20,* 775–803. doi:10.1017/S0954579408000370

Dawson, G. (2013). Dramatic increase in autism prevalence parallels explosion of research into its biology and causes. *JAMA Psychiatry, 70*(1), p. 9. doi:10.1001/jamapsychiatry.2013.488

Dawson, G., Carver, L., Meltzoff, A. N., Panagiotides, H., McPartland, J., & Webb, S. J. (2002). Neural correlates of face and object recognition in young children with autism spectrum disorder, developmental delay, and typical development. *Child Development, 73,* 700–717. doi:10.1111/1467-8624.00433

Dawson, G., Jones, E. J. H., Merkle, K., Venema, K., Lowy, R., Faja, S., . . . Webb, S. J. (2012). Early behavioral intervention is associated with normalized brain activity in young children with autism. *Journal of the American Academy of Child & Adolescent Psychiatry, 51,* 1150–1159. doi:10.1016/j.jaac.2012.08.018

Dawson, G., Munson, J., Estes, A., Osterling, J., McPartland, J., Toth, K., . . . Abbott, R. (2002). Neurocognitive function and joint attention ability in young children with autism spectrum disorder versus developmental delay. *Child Development, 73,* 345–358. doi:10.1111/1467-8624.00411

Dawson, G., & Osterling, J. (1997). Early intervention in autism: Effectiveness and common elements of current approaches. In M. J. Guralnick (Ed.), *The effectiveness of early intervention: Second generation research* (pp. 307–326). Baltimore, MD: Brookes.

Dawson, G., Rogers, S., Munson, J., Smith, M., Winter, J., Greenson, J., . . . Varley, J. (2010). Randomized, controlled trial of an intervention for toddlers with autism: The Early Start Denver Model. *Pediatrics, 125*(1), e17–e23. doi:10.1542/peds.2009-0958

Dawson, M., Mottron, L., & Gernsbacher, M. (2008). Learning in autism. In J. H. Byrne & H. L. Roediger (Eds.), *Learning and memory: A comprehensive reference: Cognitive psychology* (pp. 759–772). New York, NY: Elsevier. doi:10.1016/B978-012370509-9.00152-2

de Bruin, E. I., Ferdinand, R. F., Meester, S., de Nijs, P. F. A., & Verheij, F. (2007). High rates of psychiatric co-morbidity in PDD-NOS. *Journal of Autism and Developmental Disorders, 37,* 877–886. doi:10.1007/s10803-006-0215-x

De Lissovoy, V. (1962). Head banging in early childhood. *Child Development, 33,* 43–56.

Dietz, C., Swinkels, S., Daalen, E., Engeland, H., & Buitelaar, J. (2006). Screening for autistic spectrum disorder in children aged 14–15 months. II: Population screening with the Early Screening of Autistic Traits Questionnaire (ESAT). Design and general findings. *Journal of Autism and Developmental Disorders, 36,* 713–722. doi:10.1007/s10803-006-0114-1

Domes, G., Heinrichs, M., Michel, A., Berger, C., & Herpertz, S. C. (2007). Oxytocin improves "mind-reading" in humans. *Biological Psychiatry, 61,* 731–733. doi:10.1016/j.biopsych.2006.07.015

Drew, A., Baird, G., Baron-Cohen, S., Cox, A., Slonims, V., Wheelwright, S., . . . Charman, T. (2002). A pilot randomised control trial of a parent training intervention for pre-school children with autism. *European Child & Adolescent Psychiatry, 11,* 266–272. doi:10.1007/s00787-002-0299-6

Due, P., Holstein, B. E., Lynch, J., Diderichsen, F., Gabhain, S. N., Scheidt, P., & Currie, C. (2005). Bullying and symptoms among school-aged children: International comparative cross sectional study in 28 countries. *European Journal of Public Health, 15,* 128–132. doi:10.1093/eurpub/cki105

Dumas, J., Wolf, L., Fisman, S., & Culligan, A. (1991). Parenting stress, child behavior problems, and dysphoria in parents of children with autism, Down syndrome, behavior disorders, and normal development. *Exceptionality, 2,* 97–110. doi:10.1080/09362839109524770

Dunn, L. M., & Dunn, L. M. (1997). *Peabody Picture Vocabulary Test—III.* Circle Pines, MN: American Guidance Service.

Durand, V. M. (1990). *Severe behavior problems: A functional communication training approach.* New York, NY: Guilford Press.

Durand, V. M. (2005). Past, present and emerging directions in education. In D. Zager (Ed.), *Autism: Identification, education, and treatment* (3rd ed., pp. 89–109). Hillsdale, NJ: Erlbaum.

Durand, V. M. (2008). *When children don't sleep well: Interventions for pediatric sleep disorders, Therapist guide.* New York, NY: Oxford University Press.

Durand, V. M. (2011a, August). *The concession process: A new framework for understanding the development and treatment of challenging behavior in autism spectrum disorders.* Paper presented at the annual meeting of the American Psychological Association, Washington, DC.

Durand, V. M. (2011b). Disorders of development. In D. H. Barlow (Ed.), *Oxford handbook of clinical psychology* (pp. 551–573). New York, NY: Oxford University Press.

Durand, V. M. (2011c). *Optimistic parenting: Hope and help for you and your challenging child.* Baltimore, MD: Brookes.

Durand, V. M. (2012). Functional communication training: Treating challenging behavior. In P. A. Prelock & R. J. McCauley (Eds.), *Treatment of autism spectrum disorders: Evidence based-intervention strategies for communication and social interactions* (pp. 107–138). Baltimore, MD: Brookes.

Durand, V. M. (2013). Sleep problems in autism spectrum disorder: Assessment and treatment. In J. K. Luiselli (Ed.), *Children and youth with autism spectrum disorder (ASD): Recent advances and innovations in assessment, education, and intervention.* New York, NY: Oxford University Press.

Durand, V. M., & Barlow, D. H. (2010). *Essentials of abnormal psychology* (5th ed.). Belmont, CA: Wadsworth/Cengage Learning.

Durand, V. M., & Carr, E. G. (1987). Social influences on "self-stimulatory" behavior: Analysis and treatment application. *Journal of Applied Behavior Analysis, 20,* 119–132. doi:10.1901/jaba.1987.20-119

Durand, V. M., & Crimmins, D. B. (1988). Identifying variables maintaining self-injurious behavior. *Journal of Autism and Developmental Disorders, 18,* 99–117. doi:10.1007/BF02211821

Durand, V. M., & Hieneman, M. (2008a). *Helping parents with challenging children: Positive family intervention, Facilitator's guide.* New York, NY: Oxford University Press.

Durand, V. M., & Hieneman, M. (2008b). *Helping parents with challenging children: Positive family intervention, Workbook.* New York, NY: Oxford University Press.

Durand, V. M., Hieneman, M., Clarke, S., Wang, M., & Rinaldi, M. (2013). Positive family intervention for severe challenging behavior I: A multi-site randomized clinical trial. *Journal of Positive Behavior Interventions, 145,* 134–147. doi:10.1093/oxfordjournals.aje.a009084

Durand, V. M., & Mapstone, E. (1997). Influence of "mood-inducing" music on challenging behavior. *American Journal on Mental Retardation, 102,* 367–378. doi:10.1352/0895-8017(1998)102<0367:IOMMOC>2.0.CO;2

Durand, V. M., & Merges, E. (2009). Functional communication training to treat challenging behavior. In W. O'Donohue & J. E. Fisher (Eds.), *General principles and empirically supported techniques of cognitive behavior therapy* (pp. 320–327). New York, NY: Wiley.

Durkin, M. S., Maenner, M. J., Newschaffer, C. J., Lee, L. C., Cunniff, C. M., Daniels, J. L., . . . Zahorodny, W. (2008). Advanced parental age and the risk of autism spectrum disorder. *American Journal of Epidemiology, 168,* 1268–1276. doi:10.1093/aje/kwn250

Dykens, E. M., & Lense, M. (2011). Intellectual disabilities and autism spectrum disorder: A cautionary note. In D. G. Amaral, G. Dawson, & D. Geschwind (Eds.), *Autism spectrum disorders* (pp. 263–269). New York, NY: Oxford University Press. doi:10.1093/med/9780195371826.003.0018

Ehlers, S., Gillberg, C., & Wing, L. (1999). A screening questionnaire for Asperger syndrome and other high-functioning autism spectrum disorders in school age children. *Journal of Autism and Developmental Disorders, 29,* 129–141. doi:10.1023/A:1023040610384

Einfeld, S., & Tonge, B. J. (1989). *Developmental Behavior Checklist (DBC)*. Sydney, Australia: University of Sydney.

Eisenhower, A. S., Baker, B. L., & Blacher, J. (2005). Preschool children with intellectual disability: Syndrome specificity, behaviour problems, and maternal well-being. *Journal of Intellectual Disability Research, 49,* 657–671. doi:10.1111/j.1365-2788.2005.00699.x

Elsabbagh, M., Divan, G., Koh, Y.-J., Kim, Y. S., Kauchali, S., Marcín, C., . . . Fombonne, E. (2012). Global prevalence of autism and other pervasive developmental disorders. *Autism Research, 5,* 160–179. doi:10.1002/aur.239

Elsabbagh, M., Mercure, E., Hudry, K., Chandler, S., Pasco, G., Charman, T., . . . Johnson, Mark H. (2012). Infant neural sensitivity to dynamic eye gaze is associated with later emerging autism. *Current Biology, 22,* 338–342. doi:10.1016/j.cub.2011.12.056

Elsabbagh, M., Volein, A., Csibra, G., Holmboe, K., Garwood, H., Tucker, L., . . . Johnson, M. H. (2009). Neural correlates of eye gaze processing in the infant broader autism phenotype. *Biological Psychiatry, 65*(1), 31–38. doi:10.1016/j.biopsych.2008.09.034

Estes, A., Munson, J., Dawson, G., Koehler, E., Zhou, X.-H., & Abbott, R. (2009). Parenting stress and psychological functioning among mothers of preschool children with autism and developmental delay. *Autism, 13,* 375–387. doi:10.1177/1362361309105658

Fatemi, S., Aldinger, K., Ashwood, P., Bauman, M., Blaha, C., Blatt, G., . . . Welsh, J. (2012). Consensus paper: Pathological role of the cerebellum in autism. *The Cerebellum, 11,* 777–807. doi:10.1007/s12311-012-0355-9

Fatemi, S. H., Halt, A. R., Realmuto, G., Earle, J., Kist, D. A., Thuras, P., & Merz, A. (2002). Purkinje cell size is reduced in cerebellum of patients with autism. *Cellular and Molecular Neurobiology, 22,* 171–175. doi:10.1023/A:1019861721160

Fenske, E. C., Zalenski, S., Krantz, P. J., & McClannahan, L. E. (1985). Age at intervention and treatment outcome for autistic children in a comprehensive intervention program. *Analysis and Intervention in Developmental Disabilities, 5,* 49–58. doi:10.1016/S0270-4684(85)80005-7

Ferraioli, S. J., & Harris, S. L. (2011). Teaching joint attention to children with autism through a sibling-mediated behavioral intervention. *Behavioral Interventions, 26,* 261–281. doi:10.1002/bin.336

Ferster, C. B. (1961). Positive reinforcement and behavioral deficits of autistic children. *Child Development, 32,* 437–456.

Filipek, P. A., Accardo, P. J., Baranek, G. T., Cook, E. H., Dawson, G., Gordon, B., . . . Levy, S. E. (1999). The screening and diagnosis of autistic spectrum disorders. *Journal of Autism and Developmental Disorders, 29,* 439–484. doi:10.1023/A:1021943802493

Fombonne, E., Quirke, S., & Hagen, A. (2011). Epidemiology of pervasive developmental disorders. In D. G. Amaral, G. Dawson, & D. Geschwind (Eds.), *Autism spectrum disorders* (pp. 90–111). New York, NY: Oxford University Press. doi:10.1093/med/9780195371826.003.0007

Foster, E. M., & Pearson, E. (2012). Is inclusivity an indicator of quality of care for children with autism in special education? *Pediatrics, 130*(Suppl. 2), S179–S185. doi:10.1542/peds.2012-0900P

Fox, L., Vaughn, B. J., Wyatte, M. L., & Dunlap, G. (2002). "We can't expect other people to understand": Family perspectives on problem behavior. *Exceptional Children, 68,* 437–450.

Frances, A. (2010, February 11). Opening Pandora's box: The 19 worst suggestions for DSM–5. *Psychiatric Times, 27*(9).

Fraser, A. G., & Marcotte, E. M. (2004). A probabilistic view of gene function. *Nature Genetics, 36,* 559–564. doi:10.1038/ng1370

Frazier, T. W., Youngstrom, E. A., Speer, L., Embacher, R., Law, P., Constantino, J., . . . Eng, C. (2012). Validation of proposed DSM-5 criteria for autism spectrum disorder. *Journal of the American Academy of Child and Adolescent Psychiatry, 51*(1), 28-40. doi:10.1016/j.jaac.2011.09.021

Frith, U. (1991). Asperger and his syndrome. In U. Frith (Ed.), *Autism and Asperger syndrome* (pp. 1–36). Cambridge, England: Cambridge University Press. doi:10.1017/CBO9780511526770.001

Ganz, J. B., Earles-Vollrath, T. L., Heath, A. K., Parker, R. I., Rispoli, M. J., & Duran, J. B. (2012). A meta-analysis of single case research studies on aided augmentative and alternative communication systems with individuals with autism spectrum disorders. *Journal of Autism and Developmental Disorders, 42,* 60–74. doi:10.1007/s10803-011-1212-2

Ganz, M. L. (2007). The lifetime distribution of the incremental societal costs of autism. *Archives of Pediatrics & Adolescent Medicine, 161,* 343–349. doi:10.1001/archpedi.161.4.343

Gardener, H., Spiegelman, D., & Buka, S. L. (2011). Perinatal and neonatal risk factors for autism: A comprehensive meta-analysis. *Pediatrics, 128,* 344–355. doi:10.1542/peds.2010-1036

Gaspar de Alba, M. J., & Bodfish, J. W. (2011). Addressing parental concerns at the initial diagnosis of an autism spectrum disorder. *Research in Autism Spectrum Disorders, 5,* 633–639. doi:10.1016/j.rasd.2010.07.009

Geschwind, D. H. (2009). Advances in autism. *Annual Review of Medicine, 60*(1), 367–380. doi:10.1146/annurev.med.60.053107.121225

Ghaziuddin, M., Ghaziuddin, N., & Greden, J. (2002). Depression in persons with autism: Implications for research and clinical care. *Journal of Autism and Developmental Disorders, 32,* 299–306. doi:10.1023/A:1016330802348

Gillespie-Lynch, K., Sepeta, L., Wang, Y., Marshall, S., Gomez, L., Sigman, M., & Hutman, T. (2012). Early childhood predictors of the social competence of adults with autism. *Journal of Autism and Developmental Disorders, 42,* 161–174. doi:10.1007/s10803-011-1222-0

Gilliam, J. E. (1995). *GARS: Gilliam Autism Rating Scale: Examiner's manual.* Austin, TX: PRO-ED.

Goin-Kochel, R. P., Mackintosh, V. H., & Myers, B. J. (2009). Parental reports on the efficacy of treatments and therapies for their children with autism spectrum disorders. *Research in Autism Spectrum Disorders, 3,* 528–537. doi:10.1016/j. rasd.2008.11.001

Goin-Kochel, R. P., Myers, B. J., & Mackintosh, V. H. (2007). Parental reports on the use of treatments and therapies for children with autism-spectrum disorders. *Research in Autism Spectrum Disorders, 1,* 195–209. doi:10.1016/j. rasd.2006.08.006

Goldfarb, W. (1963). Self-awareness in schizophrenic children. *Archives of General Psychiatry, 8,* 47–60. doi:10.1001/archpsyc.1963.01720070049006

Goldman, S. E., Richdale, A., Clemons, T., & Malow, B. (2012). Parental sleep concerns in autism spectrum disorders: Variations from childhood to adolescence. *Journal of Autism and Developmental Disorders, 42,* 531–538. doi:10.1007/ s10803-011-1270-5

Goldstein, A. P., & McGinnis, E. (1997). *Skillstreaming the adolescent: New strategies and perspectives for teaching prosocial skills* (Vol. 1). Champaign, IL: Research Press.

Goldstein, H. (2002). Communication intervention for children with autism: A review of treatment efficacy. *Journal of Autism and Developmental Disorders, 32,* 373–396. doi:10.1023/A:1020589821992

Goldstein, S., & Ozonoff, S. (2008). Historical perspective and overview. In S. Goldstein, J. A. Naglieri, & S. Ozonoff (Eds.), *Assessment of autism spectrum disorders* (pp. 1–17). New York, NY: Guilford Press.

Gotham, K., Risi, S., Pickles, A., & Lord, C. (2007). The Autism Diagnostic Observation Schedule: Revised algorithms for improved diagnostic validity. *Journal of Autism and Developmental Disorders, 37,* 613–627. doi:10.1007/ s10803-006-0280-1

Grandin, T. (2011). *The way I see it: A personal look at autism and Asperger's* (2nd ed.). Arlington, TX: Future Horizons.

Green, G., Brennan, L. C., & Fein, D. (2002). Intensive behavioral treatment for a toddler at high risk for autism. *Behavior Modification, 26*(1), 69–102. doi:10.1177/0145445502026001005

Green, V. A., Pituch, K. A., Itchon, J., Choi, A., O'Reilly, M., & Sigafoos, J. (2006). Internet survey of treatments used by parents of children with autism. *Research in Developmental Disabilities, 27,* 70–84. doi:10.1016/j.ridd.2004.12.002

Greenspan, S. I., & Wieder, S. (2006). *Engaging autism: Using the floortime approach to help children relate, communicate, and think.* Cambridge, MA: Da Capo Press.

Grondhuis, S. N., & Aman, M. (2012). Assessment of anxiety in children and adolescents with autism spectrum disorders. *Research in Autism Spectrum Disorders, 6,* 1345–1365. doi:10.1016/j.rasd.2012.04.006

Guastella, A. J., Einfeld, S. L., Gray, K. M., Rinehart, N. J., Tonge, B. J., Lambert, T. J., & Hickie, I. B. (2010). Intranasal oxytocin improves emotion recognition for youth with autism spectrum disorders. *Biological Psychiatry, 67,* 692–694. doi:10.1016/j.biopsych.2009.09.020

Gunasekaran, S., & Chaplin, E. (2012). Autism spectrum disorders and offending. *Advances in Mental Health and Intellectual Disabilities, 6,* 308–313. doi:10.1108/20441281211285955

Hallmayer, J., Cleveland, S., Torres, A., Phillips, J., Cohen, B., Torigoe, T., . . . Smith, K. (2011). Genetic heritability and shared environmental factors among twin pairs with autism. *Archives of General Psychiatry, 68,* 1095–1102. doi:10.1001/archgenpsychiatry.2011.76.

Hancock, T. B., & Kaiser, A. P. (2012). Implementing enhanced milieu teaching with children who have autism spectrum disorders. In P. A. Prelock & R. J. McCauley (Eds.), *Treatment of autism spectrum disorders: Evidence based-intervention strategies for communication and social interactions* (pp. 163–187). Baltimore, MD: Brookes.

Hanley, G. P., Iwata, B. A., & McCord, B. E. (2003). Functional analysis of problem behavior: A review. *Journal of Applied Behavior Analysis, 36,* 147–185. doi:10.1901/jaba.2003.36-147

Happé, F., & Ronald, A. (2008). The "fractionable autism triad": A review of evidence from behavioural, genetic, cognitive and neural research. *Neuropsychology Review, 18,* 287–304. doi:10.1007/s11065-008-9076-8

Harris, S. L., Handleman, J., Gordon, R., Kristoff, B., & Fuentes, F. (1991). Changes in cognitive and language functioning of preschool children with autism. *Journal of Autism and Developmental Disorders, 21,* 281–290. doi:10.1007/BF02207325

Hastings, R. P. (2002). Parental stress and behaviour problems of children with developmental disability. *Journal of Intellectual and Developmental Disability, 27,* 149–160. doi:10.1080/1366825021000008657

Hastings, R. P. (2007). Longitudinal relationships between sibling behavioral adjustment and behavior problems of children with developmental disabilities. *Journal of Autism and Developmental Disorders, 37,* 1485–1492. doi:10.1007/s10803-006-0230-y

Hastings, R. P., & Brown, T. (2002). Behavior problems of children with autism, parental self-efficacy, and mental health. *American Journal on Mental*

Retardation, 107, 222–232. doi:10.1352/0895-8017(2002)107<0222:BPOCW A>2.0.CO;2

Hastings, R. P., & Johnson, E. (2001). Stress in UK families conducting intensive home-based behavioural intervention for their young child with autism. *Journal of Autism and Developmental Disorders, 31*, 327–336. doi:10.1023/A:1010799320795

Hayes, S. C., Strosahl, K. D., & Wilson, K. G. (1999). *Acceptance and commitment therapy: An experiential approach to behavior change.* New York, NY: Guilford Press.

Hedley, D., & Young, R. (2006). Social comparison processes and depressive symptoms in children and adolescents with Asperger syndrome. *Autism, 10,* 139–153. doi:10.1177/1362361306062020

Henninger, N. A., & Taylor, J. L. (2013). Outcomes in adults with autism spectrum disorders: A historical perspective. *Autism, 17,* 103–116. doi:10.1177/ 1362361312441266

Herman, G. E., Henninger, N., Ratliff-Schaub, K., Pastore, M., Fitzgerald, S., & McBride, K. L. (2007). Genetic testing in autism: How much is enough? *Genetics in Medicine, 9,* 268–274. doi:10.1097/GIM.0b013e31804d683b

Hoffman, C. D., Sweeney, D. P., Hodge, D., Lopez-Wagner, M. C., & Looney, L. (2009). Parenting stress and closeness: Mothers of typically developing children and mothers of children with autism. *Focus on Autism and Other Developmental Disabilities, 24,* 178–187. doi:10.1177/1088357609338715

Hollander, E., Novotny, S., Hanratty, M., Yaffe, R., DeCaria, C. M., Aronowitz, B. R., & Mosovich, S. (2003). Oxytocin infusion reduces repetitive behaviors in adults with autistic and Asperger's disorders. *Neuropsychopharmacology, 28,* 193–198. doi:10.1038/sj.npp.1300021

Holmes, D. (1998). *Autism through the lifespan: The Eden model.* Bethesda, MD: Woodbine House.

Honda, H., Shimizu, Y., & Rutter, M. (2005). No effect of MMR withdrawal on the incidence of autism: A total population study. *Journal of Child Psychology and Psychiatry, 46,* 572–579. doi:10.1111/j.1469-7610.2005.01425.x

Howlin, P. (2005). Outcomes in autism spectrum disorders. In F. R. Volkmar, R. Paul, A. Klin, & D. J. Cohen (Eds.), *Handbook of autism and pervasive developmental disorders* (3rd ed., pp. 201–220). New York, NY: Wiley.

Howlin, P., Magiati, I., & Charman, T. (2009). Systematic review of early intensive behavioral interventions for children with autism. *American Journal on Intellectual and Developmental Disabilities, 114*(1), 23–41.

Hoyson, M., Jamieson, B., & Strain, P. S. (1984). Individualized group instruction of normally developing and autistic-like children: The LEAP curriculum model. *Journal of Early Intervention, 8,* 157–172.

Hughes, K., Bellis, M. A., Jones, L., Wood, S., Bates, G., Eckley, L., . . . Officer, A. (2012). Prevalence and risk of violence against adults with disabilities: A systematic review and meta-analysis of observational studies. *The Lancet, 379,* 1621–1629. doi:10.1016/S0140-6736(11)61851-5

Humphrey, N., & Symes, W. (2010). Responses to bullying and use of social support among pupils with autism spectrum disorders (ASDs) in mainstream schools: A qualitative study. *Journal of Research in Special Educational Needs, 10*(2), 82–90. doi:10.1111/j.1471-3802.2010.01146.x

Hviid, A., Stellfeld, M., Wohlfahrt, J., & Melbye, M. (2003). Association between thimerosal-containing vaccine and autism. *Journal of the American Medical Association, 290,* 1763–1766. doi:10.1001/jama.290.13.1763

Hyman, S. E. (2007). Can neuroscience be integrated into the DSM-5? *Nature Reviews Neuroscience, 8,* 725–732. doi:10.1038/nrn2218

Hyman, S. L., Stewart, P. A., Schmidt, B., Lemcke, N., Foley, J. T., Peck, R., . . . Handen, B. (2012). Nutrient intake from food in children with autism. *Pediatrics, 130*(Suppl. 2), S145–S153. doi:10.1542/peds.2012-0900L

Ingersoll, B. R. (2010). Teaching social communication. *Journal of Positive Behavior Interventions, 12*(1), 33–43. doi:10.1177/1098300709334797

Interactive Autism Network. (2010). *Research report #13: From first concern to diagnosis and beyond.* Retrieved from http://www.iancommunity.org/cs/ian_research_reports/ian_research_report_13

Jacob, S., Landeros-Weisenberger, A., & Leckman, J. F. (2011). Interface between autism spectrum disorders and obsessive–compulsive behaviors: A genetic and developmental perspective. In D. G. Amaral, G. Dawson, & D. Geschwind (Eds.), *Autism spectrum disorders* (pp. 285–303). New York, NY: Oxford University Press. doi:10.1093/med/9780195371826.003.0020

Jepsen, M. I., Gray, K. M., & Taffe, J. R. (2012). Agreement in multi-informant assessment of behaviour and emotional problems and social functioning in adolescents with autistic and Asperger's disorder. *Research in Autism Spectrum Disorders, 6,* 1091–1098. doi:10.1016/j.rasd.2012.02.008

Johnson, C. P., & Myers, S. M. (2007). Identification and evaluation of children with autism spectrum disorders. *Pediatrics, 120,* 1183–1215. doi:10.1542/peds.2007-2361

Johnson, C. R., Handen, B. L., Butter, E., Wagner, A., Mulick, J., Sukhodolsky, D. G., . . . Smith, T. (2007). Development of a parent training program for children with pervasive developmental disorders. *Behavioral Interventions, 22,* 201–221. doi:10.1002/bin.237

Johnson, K. P., & Malow, B. A. (2008). Sleep in children with autism spectrum disorders. *Current Treatment Options in Neurology, 10,* 350–359. doi:10.1007/s11940-008-0038-5

Johnson, M. H., Griffin, R., Csibra, G., Halit, H., Farroni, T., De Haan, M., . . . Richards, J. (2005). The emergence of the social brain network: Evidence from typical and atypical development. *Development and Psychopathology, 17,* 599–619. doi:10.1017/S0954579405050297

Jolliffe, T., & Baron-Cohen, S. (1997). Are people with autism and Asperger syndrome faster than normal on the Embedded Figures Test? *Journal of Child Psychology and Psychiatry, 38,* 527–534. doi:10.1111/j.1469-7610.1997.tb01539.x

Jones, T. L., & Prinz, R. J. (2005). Potential roles of parental self-efficacy in parent and child adjustment: A review. *Clinical Psychology Review, 25,* 341–363. doi:10.1016/j.cpr.2004.12.004

Jordan, B. R., & Tsai, D. F. C. (2010). Whole-genome association studies for multigenic diseases: Ethical dilemmas arising from commercialization—the case of genetic testing for autism. *Journal of Medical Ethics, 36,* 440–444. doi:10.1136/jme.2009.031385

Kabat-Zinn, J. (1995). *Wherever you go, there you are: Mindfulness meditation in everyday life.* New York, NY: Hyperion.

Kaminsky, L., & Dewey, D. (2001). Siblings relationships of children with autism. *Journal of Autism and Developmental Disorders, 31,* 399–410. doi:10.1023/A:1010664603039

Kaminsky, L., & Dewey, D. (2002). Psychosocial adjustment in siblings of children with autism. *Journal of Child Psychology and Psychiatry, 43,* 225–232. doi:10.1111/1469-7610.00015

Kanne, S. M., Gerber, A., Quirmbach, L., Sparrow, S., Cicchetti, D., & Saulnier, C. (2011). The role of adaptive behavior in autism spectrum disorders: Implications for functional outcome. *Journal of Autism and Developmental Disorders, 41,* 1007–1018. doi:10.1007/s10803-010-1126-4

Kanner, L. (1943). Autistic disturbances of affective contact. *Nervous Child, 2,* 217–250.

Kanner, L. (1949). Problems of nosology and psychodynamics of early infantile autism. *American Journal of Orthopsychiatry, 19,* 416–426. doi:10.1111/j.1939-0025.1949.tb05441.x

Kanner, L. (1971). Follow-up study of eleven autistic children originally reported in 1943. *Journal of Autism and Childhood Schizophrenia, 1,* 119–145. doi:10.1007/BF01537953

Kapp, S. K., Gillespie-Lynch, K., Sherman, L. E., & Hutman, T. (2013). Deficit, difference, or both? Autism and neurodiversity. *Developmental Psychology, 49,* 59–71.

Karkhaneh, M., Clark, B., Ospina, M. B., Seida, J. C., Smith, V., & Hartling, L. (2010). Social Stories™ to improve social skills in children with autism spectrum disorder. *Autism, 14,* 641–662. doi:10.1177/1362361310373057

Kasari, C., Gulsrud, A., Freeman, S., Paparella, T., & Hellemann, G. (2012). Longitudinal follow-up of children with autism receiving targeted interventions on joint attention and play. *Journal of the American Academy of Child & Adolescent Psychiatry, 51*, 487–495. doi:10.1016/j.jaac.2012.02.019

Kaufman, A. S., & Kaufman, N. L. (2003). *Kaufman Assessment Battery for Children* (2nd ed.). Circle Pines, MN: AGS.

Kaufman, B. (1981). *A miracle to believe in.* New York, NY: Fawcett Crest.

Kaufmann, W. E., Tierney, E., Rohde, C. A., Suarez-Pedraza, M. C., Clarke, M. A., Salorio, C. F., . . . Naidu, S. (2012). Social impairments in Rett syndrome: Characteristics and relationship with clinical severity. *Journal of Intellectual Disability Research, 56*, 233–247. doi:10.1111/j.1365-2788. 2011.01404.x

Keenan, M., Henderson, M., Kerr, K. P., & Dillenburger, K. (2006). *Applied behaviour analysis and autism: Building a future together.* London, England: Kingsley.

Kim, Y. S., Leventhal, B. L., Koh, Y.-J., Fombonne, E., Laska, E., Lim, E.-C., . . . Grinker, R. R. (2011). Prevalence of autism spectrum disorders in a total population sample. *The American Journal of Psychiatry, 168*, 904–912. doi:10.1176/appi.ajp.2011.10101532

Klei, L., Sanders, S. J., Murtha, M. T., Hus, V., Lowe, J. K., Willsey, A. J., . . . Geschwind, D. (2012). Common genetic variants, acting additively, are a major source of risk for autism. *Molecular Autism, 3*(1), 1–13. doi:10.1186/ 2040-2392-3-9

Kleinhans, N. M., Johnson, L. C., Richards, T., Mahurin, R., Greenson, J., Dawson, G., & Aylward, E. (2009). Reduced neural habituation in the amygdala and social impairments in autism spectrum disorders. *The American Journal of Psychiatry, 166*, 467–475. doi:10.1176/appi.ajp.2008.07101681

Kliemann, D., Dziobek, I., Hatri, A., Baudewig, J., & Heekeren, H. R. (2012). The role of the amygdala in atypical gaze on emotional faces in autism spectrum disorders. *The Journal of Neuroscience, 32*, 9469–9476. doi:10.1523/ JNEUROSCI.5294-11.2012

Klin, A. (2011). Asperger's syndrome: From Asperger to modern day. In D. G. Amaral, G. Dawson, & D. Geschwind (Eds.), *Autism spectrum disorders* (pp. 44–59). New York, NY: Oxford University Press. doi:10.1093/med/9780195371826. 003.0004

Knapp, M. (2012). Preliminary research suggests that the overall UK cost of autism is about £34 billion each year. There needs to be a further evaluation of the economic case for early intervention. *LSE Research Online.* Retrieved from http://eprints.lse.ac.uk/44030/

Knapp, M., Romeo, R., & Beecham, J. (2009). Economic cost of autism in the UK. *Autism, 13,* 317–336. doi:10.1177/1362361309104246

Koegel, L. K., Koegel, R. L., & Smith, A. (1997). Variables related to differences in standardized test outcomes for children with autism. *Journal of Autism and Developmental Disorders, 27,* 233–243. doi:10.1023/A:1025894213424

Koegel, R., & Koegel, L. (2006). *Pivotal response treatments for autism.* Baltimore, MD: Brookes.

Koegel, R. L., & Koegel, L. K. (2012). *The PRT pocket guide: Pivotal response treatment for autism spectrum disorders.* Baltimore, MD: Brookes.

Kong, A., Frigge, M. L., Masson, G., Besenbacher, S., Sulem, P., Magnusson, G., . . . Stefansson, K. (2012). Rate of de novo mutations and the importance of father/'s age to disease risk. *Nature, 488,* 471–475. Retrieved from http://www.nature.com/nature/journal/v488/n7412/abs/nature11396.html#supplementary-information

Koning, C., Magill-Evans, J., Volden, J., & Dick, B. (2011). Efficacy of cognitive behavior therapy-based social skills intervention for school-aged boys with autism spectrum disorders. *Research in Autism Spectrum Disorders.* doi:10.1016/j.rasd.2011.07.011

Krakowiak, P., Goolin-Jones, B., Hertz-Picciotto, I., Croen, L. A., & Hansen, R. L. (2008). Sleep problems in children with autism spectrum disorders, developmental delays, and typical development: A population-based study. *Journal of Sleep Research, 17,* 197–206. doi:10.1111/j.1365-2869.2008.00650.x

Krakowiak, P., Walker, C. K., Bremer, A. A., Baker, A. S., Ozonoff, S., Hansen, R. L., & Hertz-Picciotto, I. (2012). Maternal metabolic conditions and risk for autism and other neurodevelopmental disorders. *Pediatrics, 129,* e1121–e1128. doi:10.1542/peds.2011-2583

Krug, D. A., Arick, J., & Almond, P. (1980). Behavior checklist for identifying severely handicapped individuals with high levels of autistic behavior. *Journal of Child Psychology and Psychiatry, 21*(3), 221–229. doi:10.1111/j.1469-7610.1980.tb01797.x

Kuwaik, G. A., Roberts, W., Zwaigenbaum, L., Bryson, S., Smith, I. M., Szatmari, P., . . . Brian, J. (2012). Immunization uptake in younger siblings of children with autism spectrum disorder. *Autism.* doi:10.1177/1362361312459111

La Greca, A. M. (1999). *Social Anxiety Scales for Children and Adolescents: Manual and instructions for the SASC, SASC-R, SAS-A (adolescents), and parent versions of the scales.* Miami, FL: University of Miami.

Lang, R., Rispoli, M., Machalicek, W., White, P. J., Kang, S., Pierce, N., . . . Sigafoos, J. (2009). Treatment of elopement in individuals with developmental disabilities: A systematic review. *Research in Developmental Disabilities, 30,* 670–681. doi:10.1016/j.ridd.2008.11.003

Larkin, A. S., & Gurry, S. (1998). Brief report: Progress reported in three children with autism using daily life therapy. *Journal of Autism and Developmental Disorders, 28,* 339–342. doi:10.1023/A:1026068821195

Laugeson, E. A., Frankel, F., Gantman, A., Dillon, A., & Mogil, C. (2012). Evidence-based social skills training for adolescents with autism spectrum disorders: The UCLA PEERS Program. *Journal of Autism and Developmental Disorders, 42,* 1025–1036. doi:10.1007/s10803-011-1339-1

Laugeson, E. A., Frankel, F., Mogil, C., & Dillon, A. R. (2009). Parent-assisted social skills training to improve friendships in teens with autism spectrum disorders. *Journal of Autism and Developmental Disorders, 39,* 596–606. doi:10.1007/s10803-008-0664-5

Lawton, K., & Kasari, C. (2012). Teacher-implemented joint attention intervention: Pilot randomized controlled study for preschoolers with autism. *Journal of Consulting and Clinical Psychology, 80,* 687–693. doi:10.1037/a0028506

Lecavalier, L., Leone, S., & Wiltz, J. (2006). The impact of behaviour problems on caregiver stress in young people with autism spectrum disorders. *Journal of Intellectual Disability Research, 50,* 172–183. doi:10.1111/j.1365-2788.2005.00732.x

Ledford, J. R., & Gast, D. L. (2006). Feeding problems in children with autism spectrum disorders: A review. *Focus on Autism and Other Developmental Disabilities, 21,* 153–166. doi:10.1177/10883576060210030401

Leekam, S. R., Nieto, C., Libby, S. J., Wing, L., & Gould, J. (2007). Describing the sensory abnormalities of children and adults with autism. *Journal of Autism and Developmental Disorders, 37,* 894–910. doi:10.1007/s10803-006-0218-7

Leekam, S. R., Prior, M. R., & Uljarevic, M. (2011). Restricted and repetitive behaviors in autism spectrum disorders: A review of research in the last decade. *Psychological Bulletin, 137,* 562–593. doi:10.1037/a0023341

Lehmkuhl, H. D., Storch, E. A., Bodfish, J. W., & Geffken, G. R. (2008). Brief report: Exposure and response prevention for obsessive compulsive disorder in a 12-year-old with autism. *Journal of Autism and Developmental Disorders, 38,* 977–981. doi:10.1007/s10803-007-0457-2

Leiter, R. (2002). *Leiter International Performance Scale Revised (LIPS-R).* Los Angeles, CA: Western Psychological Service.

Lewkowicz, D. J., & Hansen-Tift, A. M. (2012). Infants deploy selective attention to the mouth of a talking face when learning speech. *Proceedings of the National Academy of Sciences.* doi:10.1073/pnas.1114783109

Leyfer, O. T., Folstein, S. E., Bacalman, S., Davis, N. O., Dinh, E., Morgan, J., . . . Lainhart, J. E. (2006). Comorbid psychiatric disorders in children with autism: Interview development and rates of disorders. *Journal of Autism and Developmental Disorders, 36,* 849–861. doi:10.1007/s10803-006-0123-0

Li, X., Zou, H., & Brown, W. T. (2012). Genes associated with autism spectrum disorder. *Brain Research Bulletin, 88,* 543–552. doi:10.1016/j.brain resbull.2012.05.017

Lind, S. E., & Bowler, D. M. (2009). Delayed self-recognition in children with autism spectrum disorder. *Journal of Autism and Developmental Disorders, 39,* 643–650. doi:10.1007/s10803-008-0670-7

Lintas, C., & Persico, A. M. (2009). Autistic phenotypes and genetic testing: State-of-the-art for the clinical geneticist. *Journal of Medical Genetics, 46*(1), 1–8. doi:10.1136/jmg.2008.060871

Liu, K., & Bearman, P. S. (2012). Focal points, endogenous processes, and exogenous shocks in the autism epidemic. *Sociological Methods & Research.* doi:10.1177/0049124112460369

Lord, C., & Bishop, S. L. (2010). Autism spectrum disorders. *Social Policy Report, 24*(2), 3–21.

Lord, C., & Jones, R. M. (2012). Annual research review: Re-thinking the classification of autism spectrum disorders. *Journal of Child Psychology and Psychiatry, 53,* 490–509. doi:10.1111/j.1469-7610.2012.02547.x

Lord, C., Luyster, R., Guthrie, W., & Pickles, A. (2012). Patterns of developmental trajectories in toddlers with autism spectrum disorder. *Journal of Consulting and Clinical Psychology, 80,* 477–489. doi:10.1037/a0027214

Lord, C., Petkova, E., Hus, V., Gan, W., Lu, F., Martin, D. M., . . . Risi, S. (2012). A multisite study of the clinical diagnosis of different autism spectrum disorders. *Archives of General Psychiatry, 69,* 306–313. doi:10.1001/archgenpsychiatry.2011.148

Lord, C., Risi, S., Lambrecht, L., Cook, E. H., Leventhal, B. L., DiLavore, P. C., . . . Rutter, M. (2000). The Autism Diagnostic Observation Schedule— Generic: A standard measure of social and communication deficits associated with the spectrum of autism. *Journal of Autism and Developmental Disorders, 30*(3), 205–223. doi:10.1023/A:1005592401947

Lovaas, O. I. (1987). Behavioral treatment and normal educational and intellectual functioning in young autistic children. *Journal of Consulting and Clinical Psychology, 55,* 3–9. doi:10.1037/0022-006X.55.1.3

Lovaas, O. I., & Smith, T. (1989). A comprehensive behavioral theory of autistic children: Paradigm for research and treatment. *Journal of Behavior Therapy and Experimental Psychiatry, 20*(1), 17–29. doi:10.1016/0005-7916(89)90004-9

Lovell, B., Moss, M., & Wetherell, M. (2012). The psychosocial, endocrine and immune consequences of caring for a child with autism or ADHD. *Psychoneuro endocrinology, 37,* 534–542. doi:10.1016/j.psyneuen.2011.08.003

Luo, R., Sanders, S. J., Tian, Y., Voineagu, I., Huang, N., Chu, Su H., . . . Geschwind, Daniel H. (2012). Genome-wide transcriptome profiling reveals the functional impact of rare de novo and recurrent CNVs in autism spectrum disorders. *American Journal of Human Genetics, 91*(1), 38–55. doi:10.1016/j.ajhg.2012.05.011

Maglione, M. A., Gans, D., Das, L., Timbie, J., & Kasari, C. (2012). Nonmedical interventions for children with ASD: Recommended guidelines and further research needs. *Pediatrics, 130*(Suppl. 2), S169–S178. doi:10.1542/peds.2012-0900O

Mahler, M. (1952). On childhood psychosis and schizophrenia: Autistic and symbiotic infantile psychosis. *The Psychoanalytic Study of the Child, 7,* 286–305.

Mahoney, G., & Perales, F. (2005). Relationship-focused early intervention with children with pervasive developmental disorders and other disabilities: A comparative study. *Journal of Developmental and Behavioral Pediatrics, 26,* 77–85. doi:10.1097/00004703-200504000-00002

Mandy, W. P., & Skuse, D. H. (2008). Research Review: What is the association between the social-communication element of autism and repetitive interests, behaviours and activities? *Journal of Child Psychology and Psychiatry, 49,* 795–808. doi:10.1111/j.1469-7610.2008.01911.x

March, J. S. (1999). *Multidimensional Anxiety Scale for Children manual.* North Tonawanda, NY: Multi-Health Systems.

Matson, J. L., & Fodstad, J. C. (2009). The treatment of food selectivity and other feeding problems in children with autism spectrum disorders. *Research in Autism Spectrum Disorders, 3,* 455–461. doi:10.1016/j.rasd.2008.09.005

Mayes, S. D., & Calhoun, S. L. (2007). Learning, attention, writing, and processing speed in typical children and children with ADHD, autism, anxiety, depression, and oppositional-defiant disorder. *Child Neuropsychology, 13,* 469–493. doi:10.1080/09297040601112773

Mayes, S. D., Calhoun, S. L., Mayes, R. D., & Molitoris, S. (2012). Autism and ADHD: Overlapping and discriminating symptoms. *Research in Autism Spectrum Disorders, 6,* 277–285. doi:10.1016/j.rasd.2011.05.009

Mayes, S. D., Calhoun, S. L., Murray, M. J., Ahuja, M., & Smith, L. A. (2011). Anxiety, depression, and irritability in children with autism relative to other neuropsychiatric disorders and typical development. *Research in Autism Spectrum Disorders, 5,* 474–485. doi:10.1016/j.rasd.2010.06.012

Mayes, S. D., Calhoun, S. L., Murray, M. J., & Zahid, J. (2011). Variables associated with anxiety and depression in children with autism. *Journal of Developmental and Physical Disabilities, 23,* 325–337. doi:10.1007/s10882-011-9231-7

Mayes, S. D., Gorman, A. A., Hillwig-Garcia, J., & Syed, E. (2013). Suicide ideation and attempts in children with autism. *Research in Autism Spectrum Disorders, 7,* 109–119. doi:10.1016/j.rasd.2012.07.009

McCann, J., & Peppé, S. (2003). Prosody in autism spectrum disorders: A critical review. *International Journal of Language & Communication Disorders, 38,* 325–350. doi:10.1080/1368282031000154204

McConachie, H., Randle, V., Hammal, D., & Le Couteur, A. (2005). A controlled trial of a training course for parents of children with suspected autism spectrum disorder. *The Journal of Pediatrics, 147,* 335–340. doi:10.1016/j.jpeds.2005.03.056

McDonald, M. E., Pace, D., Blue, E., & Schwartz, D. (2012). Critical issues in causation and treatment of autism: Why fads continue to flourish. *Child & Family Behavior Therapy, 34,* 290–304. doi:10.1080/07317107.2012.732849

McEachin, J., & Leaf, R. (1999). *A work in progress: The autism partnership curriculum for discrete trial teaching with autistic children.* New York, NY: DRL Books.

McGee, G. G., Morrier, M. J., & Daly, T. (1999). An incidental teaching approach to early intervention for toddlers with autism. *Research and Practice for Persons with Severe Disabilities, 24,* 133–146. doi:10.2511/rpsd.24.3.133

McPartland, J. C., Reichow, B., & Volkmar, F. R. (2012). Sensitivity and specificity of proposed DSM-5 diagnostic criteria for autism spectrum disorder. *Journal of the American Academy of Child & Adolescent Psychiatry, 51,* 368–383. doi:10.1016/j.jaac.2012.01.007

Meirsschaut, M., Roeyers, H., & Warreyn, P. (2010). Parenting in families with a child with autism spectrum disorder and a typically developing child: Mothers' experiences and cognitions. *Research in Autism Spectrum Disorders, 4,* 661–669. doi:10.1016/j.rasd.2010.01.002

Meyer, D. J., & Vadasy, P. (1994). *Sibshops: Workshops for brothers and sisters of children with special needs.* Baltimore, MD: Brookes.

Miller, J., Bilder, D., Farley, M., Coon, H., Pinborough-Zimmerman, J., Jenson, W., . . . McMahon, W. (2013). Autism spectrum disorder reclassified: A second look at the 1980s Utah/UCLA Autism Epidemiologic Study. *Journal of Autism and Developmental Disorders, 43,* 200–210. doi:10.1007/s10803-012-1566-0

Minshew, N. J., & Keller, T. A. (2010). The nature of brain dysfunction in autism: Functional brain imaging studies. *Current Opinion in Neurology, 23,* 124–130. doi:10.1097/WCO.0b013e32833782d4

Minshew, N. J., Scherf, K. S., Behrmann, M., & Humphreys, K. (2011). Autism as a developmental neurobiological disorder: New insights from functional imaging. In D. G. Amaral, G. Dawson, & D. Geschwind (Eds.), *Autism spectrum disorders* (pp. 632–650). New York, NY: Oxford University Press. doi:10.1093/med/9780195371826.003.0041

Mirenda, P., & Iacono, T. (2009). *Autism spectrum disorders and AAC*. Baltimore, MD: Brookes.

Morrissey-Kane, E., & Prinz, R. J. (1999). Engagement in child and adolescent treatment: The role of parental cognitions and attributions. *Clinical Child and Family Psychology Review, 2*, 183–198. doi:10.1023/A:1021807106455

Mottron, L. (2011). Changing perceptions: The power of autism. *Nature, 479*, 33–35. doi:10.1038/479033a

Mullen, E. M. (1997). *Mullen scales of early learning*. Los Angeles, CA: Western Psychological Services.

Mundy, P., & Neal, A. R. (2000). Neural plasticity, joint attention, and a transactional social-orienting model of autism. *International Review of Research in Mental Retardation, 23*, 139–168

Murray, D. S., Ruble, L. A., Willis, H., & Molloy, C. A. (2009). Parent and teacher report of social skills in children with autism spectrum disorders. *Language, Speech, and Hearing Services in Schools, 40*(2), 109–115. doi:10.1044/0161-1461(2008/07-0089)

National Professional Development Center on Autism Spectrum Disorders. (2011). *Overlap between evidence-based practices identified by the National Professional Development Center on Autism Spectrum disorders and the National Standards Project*. Frank Porter Graham Child Development Institute, University of North Carolina at Chapel Hill.

National Research Council, Committee on Educational Interventions for Children With Autism. (2001). *Educating children with autism*. Washington, DC: National Academy Press.

Neale, B. M., Kou, Y., Liu, L., Ma'ayan, A., Samocha, K. E., Sabo, A., . . . Makarov, V. (2012). Patterns and rates of exonic de novo mutations in autism spectrum disorders. *Nature, 485*, 242–245. doi:10.1038/nature11011

Neul, J. L., Kaufmann, W. E., Glaze, D. G., Christodoulou, J., Clarke, A. J., Bahi-Buisson, N., . . . Zappella, M. (2010). Rett syndrome: Revised diagnostic criteria and nomenclature. *Annals of Neurology, 68*, 944–950. doi:10.1002/ana.22124

Newman, S. S., & Ghaziuddin, M. (2008). Violent crime in Asperger syndrome: The role of psychiatric comorbidity. *Journal of Autism and Developmental Disorders, 38*, 1848–1852. doi:10.1007/s10803-008-0580-8

Nikopoulos, C. K., & Keenan, M. (2004). Effects of video modeling on social initiations by children with autism. *Journal of Applied Behavior Analysis, 37*, 93–96. doi:10.1901/jaba.2004.37-93

Odom, S. L., Boyd, B. A., Hall, L. J., & Hume, K. (2010). Evaluation of comprehensive treatment models for individuals with autism spectrum disorders. *Journal of Autism and Developmental Disorders, 40,* 425–436. doi:10.1007/s10803-009-0825-1

Odom, S. L., Collet-Klingenberg, L., Rogers, S. J., & Hatton, D. D. (2010). Evidence-based practices in interventions for children and youth with autism spectrum disorders. *Preventing School Failure: Alternative Education for Children and Youth, 54,* 275–282. doi:10.1080/10459881003785506

O'Neill, R. E., Horner, R. H., Albin, R. W., Storey, K., & Sprague, J. R. (1990). *Functional analysis: A practical assessment guide.* Sycamore, IL: Sycamore.

Oppenheim-Leaf, M. L., Leaf, J. B., Dozier, C., Sheldon, J. B., & Sherman, J. A. (2012). Teaching typically developing children to promote social play with their siblings with autism. *Research in Autism Spectrum Disorders, 6,* 777–791. doi:10.1016/j.rasd.2011.10.010

Orsmond, G. I., Krauss, M., & Seltzer, M. M. (2004). Peer relationships and social and recreational activities among adolescents and adults with autism. *Journal of Autism and Developmental Disorders, 34,* 245–256. doi:10.1023/B:JADD.0000029547.96610.df

Owens, J. A., Spirito, A., & McGuinn, M. (2000). The Children's Sleep Habits Questionnaire (CSHQ): Psychometric properties of a survey instrument for school-aged children. *Sleep, 23,* 1043–1052.

Ozonoff, S., & Cathcart, K. (1998). Effectiveness of a home program intervention for young children with autism. *Journal of Autism and Developmental Disorders, 28,* 25–32. doi:10.1023/A:1026006818310

Ozonoff, S., Heung, K., Byrd, R., Hansen, R., & Hertz-Picciotto, I. (2008). The onset of autism: Patterns of symptom emergence in the first years of life. *Autism Research, 1,* 320–328. doi:10.1002/aur.53

Ozonoff, S., Iosif, A. M., Baguio, F., Cook, I. C., Hill, M. M., Hutman, T., . . . Sigman, M. (2010). A prospective study of the emergence of early behavioral signs of autism. *Journal of the American Academy of Child & Adolescent Psychiatry, 49,* 256–266.

Ozonoff, S., & Miller, J. (1995). Teaching theory of mind: A new approach to social skills training for individuals with autism. *Journal of Autism and Developmental Disorders, 25,* 415–433. doi:10.1007/BF02179376

Ozonoff, S., Young, G. S., Carter, A., Messinger, D., Yirmiya, N., Zwaigenbaum, L., . . . Stone, W. L. (2011). Recurrence risk for autism spectrum disorders: A Baby Siblings Research Consortium study. *Pediatrics, 128,* e488–e495. doi:10.1542/peds.2010-2825

Paclawskyj, T. R., Matson, J. L., Rush, K. S., Smalls, Y., & Vollmer, T. R. (2000). Questions about behavioral function (QABF): A behavioral checklist for functional assessment of aberrant behavior. *Research in Developmental Disabilities, 21,* 223–229. doi:10.1016/S0891-4222(00)00036-6

Panerai, S., Ferrante, L., & Zingale, M. (2002). Benefits of the treatment and education of autistic and communication handicapped children (TEACCH) programme as compared with a non-specific approach. *Journal of Intellectual Disability Research, 46,* 318–327. doi:10.1046/j.1365-2788.2002.00388.x

Parner, E. T., Baron-Cohen, S., Lauritsen, M. B., Jørgensen, M., Schieve, L. A., Yeargin-Allsopp, M., & Obel, C. (2012). Parental age and autism spectrum disorders. *Annals of Epidemiology, 22,* 143–150. doi:10.1016/j.annepidem.2011.12.006

Patterson, S. Y., Smith, V., & Mirenda, P. (2012). A systematic review of training programs for parents of children with autism spectrum disorders: Single subject contributions. *Autism, 16,* 498–522. doi:10.1177/1362361311413398

Paul, R., Augustyn, A., Klin, A., & Volkmar, F. R. (2005). Perception and production of prosody by speakers with autism spectrum disorders. *Journal of Autism and Developmental Disorders, 35,* 205–220. doi:10.1007/s10803-004-1999-1

Pellicano, E., Maybery, M., Durkin, K., & Maley, A. (2006). Multiple cognitive capabilities/deficits in children with an autism spectrum disorder: "Weak" central coherence and its relationship to theory of mind and executive control. *Development and Psychopathology, 18*(1), 77–98. doi:10.1017/S0954579406060056

Pellicano, E., & Stears, M. (2011). Bridging autism, science and society: Moving toward an ethically informed approach to autism research. *Autism Research, 4,* 271–282. doi:10.1002/aur.201

Persico, A. M., & Bourgeron, T. (2006). Searching for ways out of the autism maze: Genetic, epigenetic and environmental clues. *Trends in Neurosciences, 29,* 349–358. doi:10.1016/j.tins.2006.05.010

Peters-Scheffer, N., Didden, R., Korzilius, H., & Sturmey, P. (2011). A meta-analytic study on the effectiveness of comprehensive ABA-based early intervention programs for children with autism spectrum disorders. *Research in Autism Spectrum Disorders, 5*(1), 60–69. doi:10.1016/j.rasd.2010.03.011

Pfiffner, L. J., Kaiser, N. M., Burner, C., Zalecki, C., Rooney, M., Setty, P., & McBurnett, K. (2011). From clinic to school: Translating a collaborative school-home behavioral intervention for ADHD. *School Mental Health, 3,* 127–142. doi:10.1007/s12310-011-9059-4

Pilowsky, T., Yirmiya, N., Doppelt, O., Gross-Tsur, V., & Shalev, R. S. (2004). Social and emotional adjustment of siblings of children with autism. *Journal of Child Psychology and Psychiatry, 45,* 855–865. doi:10.1111/j.1469-7610.2004.00277.x

Plaisted, K., O'Riordan, M., & Baron-Cohen, S. (1998). Enhanced visual search for a conjunctive target in autism: A research note. *Journal of Child Psychology and Psychiatry, 39,* 777–783. doi:10.1017/S0021963098002613

Plotkin, S., Gerber, J. S., & Offit, P. A. (2009). Vaccines and autism: A tale of shifting hypotheses. *Clinical Infectious Diseases, 48,* 456–461. doi:10.1086/596476

Poon, K. K., Watson, L., Baranek, G., & Poe, M. (2012). To what extent do joint attention, imitation, and object play behaviors in infancy predict later communication and intellectual functioning in ASD? *Journal of Autism and Developmental Disorders, 42,* 1064–1074. doi:10.1007/s10803-011-1349-z

Post, M., Haymes, L., Storey, K., Loughrey, T., & Campbell, C. (2012). Understanding stalking behaviors by individuals with autism spectrum disorders and recommended prevention strategies for school settings. *Journal of Autism and Developmental Disorders,* 1–9. doi:10.1007/s10803-012-1712-8

Pringle, B. A., Colpe, L. J., Blumberg, S. J., Avila, R. M., & Kogan, M. D. (2012). *Diagnostic history and treatment of school-aged children with autism spectrum disorder and special health care needs* (NCHS Data Brief No. 97). Hyattsville, MD: National Center for Health Statistics.

Prizant, B., Wetherby, A., Rubin, E., Laurent, A., & Rydell, P. (2006). *The SCERTS model: A comprehensive educational approach for children with autism spectrum disorders.* Baltimore, MD: Brookes.

Rao, P. A., Beidel, D., & Murray, M. (2008). Social skills interventions for children with Asperger's syndrome or high-functioning autism: A review and recommendations. *Journal of Autism and Developmental Disorders, 38,* 353–361. doi:10.1007/s10803-007-0402-4

Rao, P. A., & Beidel, D. C. (2009). The impact of children with high-functioning autism on parental stress, sibling adjustment, and family functioning. *Behavior Modification, 33,* 437–451. doi:10.1177/0145445509336427

Reaven, J. A., Blakeley-Smith, A., Culhane-Shelburne, K., & Hepburn, S. (2012). Group cognitive behavior therapy for children with high-functioning autism spectrum disorders and anxiety: A randomized trial. *Journal of Child Psychology and Psychiatry, 53,* 410–419. doi:10.1111/j.1469-7610.2011.02486.x

Reaven, J. A., Blakeley-Smith, A., Nichols, S., & Hepburn, S. (2011). *Facing your fears: Group therapy for managing anxiety in children with high-functioning autism spectrum disorders (facilitator's manual).* Baltimore, MD: Brookes.

Reaven, J. A., & Hepburn, S. (2003). Cognitive–behavioral treatment of obsessive–compulsive disorder in a child with Asperger syndrome: A case report. *Autism, 7,* 145–164. doi:10.1177/1362361303007002003

Reaven, J. A., & Hepburn, S. (2006). The parent's role in the treatment of anxiety symptoms in children with high-functioning autism spectrum disorders. *Mental Health Aspects of Developmental Disabilities. 9*(3), 73–81.

Reichenberg, A., Gross, R., Weiser, M., Bresnahan, M., Silverman, J., Harlap, S., . . . Lubin, G. (2006). Advancing paternal age and autism. *Archives of General Psychiatry, 63,* 1026–1032. doi:10.1001/archpsyc.63.9.1026

Reichow, B., & Wolery, M. (2009). Comprehensive synthesis of early intensive behavioral interventions for young children with autism based on the UCLA young autism project model. *Journal of Autism and Developmental Disorders, 39,* 23–41. doi:10.1007/s10803-008-0596-0

Remington, A., Campbell, R., & Swettenham, J. (2012). Attentional status of faces for people with autism spectrum disorder. *Autism, 16,* 59–73. doi:10.1177/1362361311409257

Research Units on Pediatric Psychopharmacology (RUPP) Autism Network. (2005). Randomized, controlled, crossover trial of methylphenidate in pervasive developmental disorders with hyperactivity. *Archives of General Psychiatry, 62,* 1266–1274. doi:10.1001/archpsyc.62.11.1266

Reynolds, C. R., & Kamphaus, R. W. (1998). *Behavior assessment system for children.* Circle Pines, MN: American Guidance Service.

Richdale, A. L., & Schreck, K. A. (2009). Sleep problems in autism spectrum disorders: Prevalence, nature, & possible biopsychosocial aetiologies. *Sleep Medicine Reviews, 13,* 403–411. doi:10.1016/j.smrv.2009.02.003

Robins, D. L., Fein, D., Barton, M. L., & Green, J. A. (2001). The Modified Checklist for Autism in Toddlers: An initial study investigating the early detection of autism and pervasive developmental disorders. *Journal of Autism and Developmental Disorders, 31,* 131–144. doi:10.1023/A:1010738829569

Rogers, S. J., Hayden, D., Hepburn, S., Charlifue-Smith, R., Hall, T., & Hayes, A. (2006). Teaching young nonverbal children with autism useful speech: A pilot study of the Denver model and PROMPT interventions. *Journal of Autism and Developmental Disorders, 36,* 1007–1024. doi:10.1007/s10803-006-0142-x

Rogers, S. J., & Vismara, L. A. (2008). Evidence-based comprehensive treatments for early autism. *Journal of Clinical Child and Adolescent Psychology, 37,* 8–38. doi:10.1080/15374410701817808

Roid, G. H. (2003). *Stanford–Binet Intelligence Scales, Fifth edition (SB5).* Rolling Meadows, IL: Riverside.

Rojahn, J., Matson, J. L., Lott, D., Esbensen, A. J., & Smalls, Y. (2001). The Behavior Problems Inventory: An instrument for the assessment of self-injury, stereotyped behavior, and aggression/destruction in individuals with developmental disabilities. *Journal of Autism and Developmental Disorders, 31,* 577–588. doi:10.1023/A:1013299028321

Ross, C. A., & Tabrizi, S. J. (2011). Huntington's disease: From molecular pathogenesis to clinical treatment. *The Lancet Neurology, 10,* 83–98. doi:10.1016/S1474-4422(10)70245-3

Rozga, A., Hutman, T., Young, G., Rogers, S., Ozonoff, S., Dapretto, M., & Sigman, M. (2011). Behavioral profiles of affected and unaffected siblings of children with autism: Contribution of measures of mother–infant interaction and nonverbal communication. *Journal of Autism and Developmental Disorders, 41,* 287–301. doi:10.1007/s10803-010-1051-6

Rutter, M. (2011a). Progress in understanding autism: 2007–2010. *Journal of Autism and Developmental Disorders, 41,* 395–404. doi:10.1007/s10803-011-1184-2

Rutter, M. (2011b). Research review: Child psychiatric diagnosis and classification: Concepts, findings, challenges and potential. *Journal of Child Psychology and Psychiatry, 52,* 647–660. doi:10.1111/j.1469-7610.2011.02367.x

Rutter, M., Bailey, A., Bolton, P., & Couteur, A. (1994). Autism and known medical conditions: Myth and substance. *Journal of Child Psychology and Psychiatry, 35,* 311–322. doi:10.1111/j.1469-7610.1994.tb01164.x

Rutter, M., Bailey, A., & Lord, C. (2003). *The Social Communication Questionnaire: Manual.* Los Angeles, CA: Western Psychological Services.

Rutter, M., Le Couteur, A., & Lord, C. (2003). *Autism Diagnostic Interview— Revised.* Los Angeles, CA: Western Psychological Services.

Ryan, S., & Cole, K. R. (2009). From advocate to activist? Mapping the experiences of mothers of children on the autism spectrum. *Journal of Applied Research in Intellectual Disabilities, 22*(1), 43–53. doi:10.1111/j.1468-3148.2008.00438.x

Sanders, S. J., Murtha, M. T., Gupta, A. R., Murdoch, J. D., Raubeson, M. J., Willsey, A. J., . . . State, M. W. (2012). *De novo* mutations revealed by whole-exome sequencing are strongly associated with autism. *Nature, 485, 237–241.*

Sandler, A. (2005). Placebo effects in developmental disabilities: Implications for research and practice. *Mental Retardation and Developmental Disabilities Research Reviews, 11,* 164–170. doi:10.1002/mrdd.20065

Scheeren, A. M., de Rosnay, M., Koot, H. M., & Begeer, S. (2013). Rethinking theory of mind in high-functioning autism spectrum disorder. *Journal of Child Psychology and Psychiatry, 54,* 628–635.

Schietecatte, I., Roeyers, H., & Warreyn, P. (2012). Exploring the nature of joint attention impairments in young children with autism spectrum disorder: Associated social and cognitive skills. *Journal of Autism and Developmental Disorders, 42,* 1–12. doi:10.1007/s10803-011-1209-x

Schopler, E., Reichler, R. J., & Renner, B. R. (1986). *The Childhood Autism Rating Scale (CARS): For diagnostic screening and classification of autism:* New York, NY: Irvington.

Schreck, K. A. (2001). Behavioral treatments for sleep problems in autism: Empirically supported or just universally accepted? *Behavioral Interventions, 16,* 265–278. doi:10.1002/bin.98

Schultz, T. R., Schmidt, C. T., & Stichter, J. P. (2011). A review of parent education programs for parents of children with autism spectrum disorders. *Focus on Autism and Other Developmental Disabilities, 26,* 96–104. doi:10.1177/1088357610397346

Schumann, C. M., & Amaral, D. G. (2006). Stereological analysis of amygdala neuron number in autism. *The Journal of Neuroscience, 26,* 7674–7679. doi:10.1523/JNEUROSCI.1285-06.2006

Schwarz, S. M. (2003). Feeding disorders in children with developmental disabilities. *Infants and Young Children, 16,* 317–330. doi:10.1097/00001163-200310000-00005

Scott, F. J., Baron-Cohen, S., Bolton, P., & Brayne, C. (2002). The CAST (Childhood Asperger Syndrome Test): Preliminary development of a UK screen for mainstream primary-school-age children. *Autism, 6,* 9–31. doi:10.1177/1362361302006001003

Sebat, J., Lakshmi, B., Malhotra, D., Troge, J., Lese-Martin, C., Walsh, T., . . . Kendall, J. (2007). Strong association of de novo copy number mutations with autism. *Science, 316,* 445–449. doi:10.1126/science.1138659

Segal, Z. V., Williams, J. M. G., & Teasdale, J. D. (2012). *Mindfulness-based cognitive therapy for depression.* New York, NY: Guilford Press.

Seidman, I., Yirmiya, N., Milshtein, S., Ebstein, R., & Levi, S. (2012). The Broad Autism Phenotype Questionnaire: Mothers versus fathers of children with an autism spectrum disorder. *Journal of Autism and Developmental Disorders, 42,* 837–846. doi:10.1007/s10803-011-1315-9

Seligman, M. E. (1998). *Learned optimism: How to change your mind and your life.* New York, NY: Pocket Books.

Seligman, M. E., Abramson, L. Y., Semmel, A., & Von Baeyer, C. (1979). Depressive attributional style. *Journal of Abnormal Psychology, 88,* 242–247. doi:10.1037/0021-843X.88.3.242

Seltzer, M. M., Greenberg, J. S., Hong, J., Smith, L. E., Almeida, D. M., Coe, C., & Stawski, R. S. (2010). Maternal cortisol levels and behavior problems in adolescents and adults with ASD. *Journal of Autism and Developmental Disorders, 40,* 457–469. doi:10.1007/s10803-009-0887-0

Sharma, S., Woolfson, L. M., & Hunter, S. C. (2012). Confusion and inconsistency in diagnosis of Asperger syndrome: A review of studies from 1981 to 2010. *Autism, 16,* 465–486. doi:10.1177/1362361311411935

Sharp, W. G., Berry, R. C., McCracken, C., Nuhu, N. N., Marvel, E., Saulnier, C. A., . . . Jaquess, D. L. (2013). Feeding problems and nutrient intake in children with autism spectrum disorders: A meta-analysis and comprehensive review of the literature. *Journal of Autism and Developmental Disorders.* Advance online publication. doi:10.1007/s10803-013-1771-5

Shelton, J. F., Hertz-Picciotto, I., & Pessah, I. N. (2012). Tipping the balance of autism risk: Potential mechanisms linking pesticides and autism. *Environmental Health Perspectives, 120,* 944–951. doi:10.1289/ehp.1104553

Shen, Y., Dies, K. A., Holm, I. A., Bridgemohan, C., Sobeih, M. M., Caronna, E. B., . . . Miller, D. T. (2010). Clinical genetic testing for patients with autism spectrum disorders. *Pediatrics, 125,* e727–e735. doi:10.1542/peds.2009-1684

Shriberg, L. D., Paul, R., McSweeny, J. L., Klin, A., Cohen, D. J., & Volkmar, F. R. (2001). Speech and prosody characteristics of adolescents and adults with high-functioning autism and Asperger syndrome. *Journal of Speech, Language, and Hearing Research, 44,* 1097–1115. doi:10.1044/1092-4388(2001/087)

Siegel, M., & Beaulieu, A. A. (2012). Psychotropic medications in children with autism spectrum disorders: A systematic review and synthesis for evidence-based practice. *Journal of Autism and Developmental Disorders, 42,* 1592–1605.

Silverman, J. M., Smith, C. J., Schmeidler, J., Hollander, E., Lawlor, B. A., Fitzgerald, M., . . . Galvin, P. (2002). Symptom domains in autism and related conditions: Evidence for familiality. *American Journal of Medical Genetics, 114*(1), 64–73. doi:10.1002/ajmg.10048

Simpson, R. L., de Boer-Ott, S. R., & Smith-Myles, B. (2003). Inclusion of learners with autism spectrum disorders in general education settings. *Topics in Language Disorders, 23,* 116–133. doi:10.1097/00011363-200304000-00005

Singer, J. (1999). "Why can't you be normal for once in your life?" From a "problem with no name" to the emergence of a new category of difference. In M. Corker & S. French (Eds.), *Disability discourse* (pp. 59–67). Buckingham, England: Open University Press.

Sivertsen, B., Posserud, M.-B., Gillberg, C., Lundervold, A. J., & Hysing, M. (2012). Sleep problems in children with autism spectrum problems: A longitudinal population-based study. *Autism, 16,* 139–150. doi:10.1177/1362361311404255

Smith, L. E., Hong, J., Seltzer, M. M., Greenberg, J., Almeida, D., & Bishop, S. (2010). Daily experiences among mothers of adolescents and adults with autism spectrum disorder. *Journal of Autism and Developmental Disorders, 40,* 167–178. doi:10.1007/s10803-009-0844-y

Smith, T. (2001). Discrete trial training in the treatment of autism. *Focus on Autism and Other Developmental Disabilities, 16,* 86–92. doi:10.1177/108835760101600204

Solish, A., & Perry, A. (2008). Parents' involvement in their children's behavioral intervention programs: Parent and therapist perspectives. *Research in Autism Spectrum Disorders, 2,* 728–738. doi:10.1016/j.rasd.2008.03.001

Sparrow, S., Cicchetti, D., & Balla, D. (2005). *Vineland-II. Vineland Adaptive Behavior Scales. Survey forms manual.* Minneapolis, MN: NCS Pearson.

Spratt, E. G., Nicholas, J., Brady, K., Carpenter, L., Hatcher, C., Meekins, K., . . . Charles, J. (2012). Enhanced cortisol response to stress in children in autism. *Journal of Autism and Developmental Disorders, 42,* 75–81. doi:10.1007/ s10803-011-1214-0

Stahmer, A. C., & Ingersoll, B. (2004). Inclusive programming for toddlers with autism spectrum disorders: Outcomes from the Children's Toddler School. *Journal of Positive Behavior Interventions, 6,* 67–82. doi:10.1177/1098300704 0060020201

Staples, A. D., & Bates, J. E. (2011). Children's sleep deficits and cognitive and behavioral adjustment. In M. El-Sheikh (Ed.), *Sleep and development: Familial and socio-cultural considerations* (pp. 133–164). New York, NY: Oxford University Press.

Steed, E. A., & Durand, V. M. (2013). Optimistic teaching: Improving the capacity for teachers to reduce young children's challenging behavior. *School Mental Health, 5,* 15–24. doi:10.1007/s12310-012-9084-y

Stehr-Green, P., Tull, P., Stellfeld, M., Mortenson, P. B., & Simpson, D. (2003). Autism and thimerosal-containing vaccines: Lack of consistent evidence for an association. *American Journal of Preventive Medicine, 25,* 101–106. doi:10.1016/ S0749-3797(03)00113-2

Steiner, A., Goldsmith, T., Snow, A., & Chawarska, K. (2012). Practitioner's guide to assessment of autism spectrum disorders in infants and toddlers. *Journal of Autism and Developmental Disorders, 42,* 1183–1196. doi:10.1007/s10803-011-1376-9

Stokes, M., & Newton, N. (2004). Autism spectrum disorders and stalking. *Autism, 8,* 337–339.

Stokes, M., Newton, N., & Kaur, A. (2007). Stalking, and social and romantic functioning among adolescents and adults with autism spectrum disorder. *Journal of Autism and Developmental Disorders, 37,* 1969–1986. doi:10.1007/ s10803-006-0344-2

Stone, W. L., Coonrod, E., & Ousley, O. (2000). Brief report: Screening Tool for Autism in Two-Year-Olds (STAT): Development and preliminary data. *Journal of Autism and Developmental Disorders, 30,* 607–612. doi:10.1023/A:1005647629002

Stone, W. L., Ruble, L., Coonrod, E., Hepburn, S., & Pennington, M. (2003). *TRIAD social skills assessment manual.* Nashville, TN: Medical Center South..

Swartz, J. R., Wiggins, J. L., Carrasco, M., Lord, C., & Monk, C. S. (2013). Amygdala habituation and prefrontal functional connectivity in youth with autism spectrum disorders. *Journal of the American Academy of Child & Adolescent Psychiatry, 52*(1), 84–93. doi:10.1016/j.jaac.2012.10.012

Szatmari, P. (2011). Is autism, at least in part, a disorder of fetal programming? *Archives of General Psychiatry, 68,* 1091–1092. doi:10.1001/archgenpsychiatry. 2011.99

Szatmari, P., & McConnell, B. (2011). Anxiety and mood disorders in individuals with autism spectrum disorder. In D. G. Amaral, G. Dawson, & D. Geschwind (Eds.), *Autism spectrum disorders* (pp. 330–338). New York, NY: Oxford University Press. doi:10.1093/med/9780195371826.003.0023

Tansey, K. E., Brookes, K. J., Hill, M. J., Cochrane, L. E., Gill, M., Skuse, D., . . . Anney, R. J. L. (2010). Oxytocin receptor (OXTR) does not play a major role in the aetiology of autism: Genetic and molecular studies. *Neuroscience Letters, 474,* 163–167. doi:10.1016/j.neulet.2010.03.035

Taylor, B. P., & Hollander, E. (2011). Comorbid obsessive-compulsive disorders. In D. G. Amaral, G. Dawson, & D. Geschwind (Eds.), *Autism spectrum disorders* (pp. 270–284). New York, NY: Oxford University Press. doi:10.1093/med/9780195371826.003.0019

Test, D. W., Richter, S., Knight, V., & Spooner, F. (2011). A comprehensive review and meta-analysis of the social stories literature. *Focus on Autism and Other Developmental Disabilities, 26*(1), 49–62. doi:10.1177/1088357609351573

Thomeer, M. L., Lopata, C., Volker, M. A., Toomey, J. A., Lee, G. K., Smerbeck, A. M., . . . Smith, R. A. (2012). Randomized clinical trial replication of a psychosocial treatment for children with high-functioning autism spectrum disorders. *Psychology in the Schools, 49,* 942–954. doi:10.1002/pits.21647

Thompson, J. R., Bradley, V. J., Buntinx, W. H. E., Schalock, R. L., Shogren, K. A., Snell, M. E., . . . Yeager, M. H. (2009). Conceptualizing supports and the support needs of people with intellectual disability. *Intellectual and Developmental Disabilities, 47,* 135–146. doi:10.1352/1934-9556-47.2.135

Tinbergen, E. A., & Tinbergen, N. (1972). *Early childhood autism: An ethological approach.* Berlin, Germany: Parey.

Tincani, M., & Devis, K. (2011). Quantitative synthesis and component analysis of single-participant studies on the Picture Exchange Communication System. *Remedial and Special Education, 32,* 458–470. doi:10.1177/0741932510362494

Tsao, L.-L., Davenport, R., & Schmiege, C. (2012). Supporting siblings of children with autism spectrum disorders. *Early Childhood Education Journal, 40*(1), 47–54. doi:10.1007/s10643-011-0488-3

Tuchman, R. (2011). Epilepsy and encephalography in autism spectrum disorders. In D. G. Amaral, G. Dawson, & D. Geschwind (Eds.), *Autism spectrum disorders* (pp. 381–394). New York, NY: Oxford University Press. doi:10.1093/med/9780195371826.003.0026

Turnbull, A., & Turnbull, R. (2011). Right science and right results: Lifestyle change, PBS, and human dignity. *Journal of Positive Behavior Interventions, 13*(2), 69–77. doi:10.1177/1098300710385347 van den Heuvel, O. A., Veltman, D. J., Groenewegen, H. J., Dolan, R. J., Cath, D. C., Boellaard, R., . . . van Dyck, R. (2004). Amygdala activity in obsessive-compulsive disorder with contamination fear: A study with oxygen-15 water positron emission tomography. *Psychiatry Research: Neuroimaging, 132,* 225–237. doi:10.1016/j.pscychresns.2004.06.007

van der Meer, L., Sutherland, D., O'Reilly, M. F., Lancioni, G. E., & Sigafoos, J. (2012). A further comparison of manual signing, picture exchange, and speech-generating devices as communication modes for children with autism spectrum disorders. *Research in Autism Spectrum Disorders, 6,* 1247–1257. doi:10.1016/j.rasd.2012.04.005

Van Roekel, E., Scholte, R. H. J., & Didden, R. (2010). Bullying among adolescents with autism spectrum disorders: Prevalence and perception. *Journal of Autism and Developmental Disorders, 40,* 63–73. doi:10.1007/s10803-009-0832-2

Volk, H. E., Lurmann, F., Penfold, B., Hertz-Picciotto, I., & McConnell, R. (2013). Traffic-related air pollution, particulate matter, and autism. *JAMA Psychiatry, 70,* 71–77. doi:10.1001/jamapsychiatry.2013.266

Volkmar, F. R. (1992). Childhood disintegrative disorder: Issues for DSM–IV. *Journal of Autism and Developmental Disorders, 22,* 625–642. doi:10.1007/BF01046331

Volkmar, F. R., Klin, A., Schultz, R. T., & State, M. W. (2009). Pervasive developmental disorders. In B. J. Sadock, V. A. Sadock, & P. Ruiz (Eds.), *Kaplan & Sadock's comprehensive textbook of psychiatry* (9th ed., Vol. II, pp. 3540–3559). Philadelphia, PA: Lippincott Williams & Wilkins.

Volpe, R. J., Young, G. I., Piana, M. G., & Zaslofsky, A. F. (2012). Integrating classwide early literacy intervention and behavioral supports a pilot investigation. *Journal of Positive Behavior Interventions, 14*(1), 56–64. doi:10.1177/1098300711402591

Voos, A. C., Pelphrey, K., Tirrell, J., Bolling, D., Wyk, B., Kaiser, M., . . . Ventola, P. (2013). Neural mechanisms of improvements in social motivation after pivotal response treatment: Two case studies. *Journal of Autism and Developmental Disorders, 43,* 1–10. doi:10.1007/s10803-012-1683-9

Vriend, J. L., Corkum, P. V., Moon, E. C., & Smith, I. M. (2011). Behavioral interventions for sleep problems in children with autism spectrum disorders: Current findings and future directions. *Journal of Pediatric Psychology, 36,* 1017–1029. doi:10.1093/jpepsy/jsr044

Wakefield, A. J., Murch, S. H., Anthony, A., Linnell, J., Casson, D. M., Malik, M., . . . Walker-Smith, J. A. (1998). RETRACTED: Ileal-lymphoid-nodular hyperplasia, non-specific colitis, and pervasive developmental disorder in children. *Lancet, 351,* 637–641. doi:10.1016/S0140-6736(97)11096-0

Walton, K. M., & Ingersoll, B. R. (2012). Evaluation of a sibling-mediated imitation intervention for young children with autism. *Journal of Positive Behavior Interventions, 14,* 241–253. doi:10.1177/1098300712437044

Wang, L. W., Tancredi, D. J., & Thomas, D. W. (2011). The prevalence of gastrointestinal problems in children across the United States with autism spectrum disorders from families with multiple affected members. *Journal of Developmental and Behavioral Pediatrics, 32,* 351–360. doi:10.1097/DBP.0b013e31821bd06a

Wapner, R. (2012). A multicenter, prospective, masked comparison of chromosomal microarray with standard karyotyping for routine and high risk prenatal diagnosis. *American Journal of Obstetrics and Gynecology, 206*(1, Suppl.), S2. doi:10.1016/j.ajog.2011.10.027

Warren, Z., McPheeters, M. L., Sathe, N., Foss-Feig, J. H., Glasser, A., & Veenstra-VanderWeele, J. (2011). A systematic review of early intensive intervention for autism spectrum disorders. *Pediatrics, 127,* e1303–e1311. doi:10.1542/peds.2011-0426

Warren, Z., & Stone, W. L. (2011). Best practices: Early diagnosis and psychological assessment. In D. G. Amaral, G. Dawson, & D. Geschwind (Eds.), *Autism spectrum disorders* (pp. 1271–1282). New York, NY: Oxford University Press. doi:10.1093/med/9780195371826.003.0082

Wechsler, D. (2002). *Wechsler Preschool and Primary Scale of Intelligence* (3rd ed.). San Antonio, TX: Harcourt Assessment.

Wechsler, D. (2003). *Wechsler Intelligence Scale for Children* (4th ed.). San Antonio, TX: Psychological Corporation.

Wechsler, D. (2008). *Wechsler Adult Intelligence Scale* (4th ed.). San Antonio, TX: Harcourt Assessment.

Wegner, J. R. (2012). Augmentative and alternative communication strategies: Manual signs, picture communication, and speech-generating devices. In P. A. Prelock & R. J. McCauley (Eds.), *Treatment of autism spectrum disorders: Evidence based-intervention strategies for communication and social interactions* (pp. 27–48). Baltimore, MD: Brookes.

Wermter, A.-K., Kamp-Becker, I., Hesse, P., Schulte-Körne, G., Strauch, K., & Remschmidt, H. (2010). Evidence for the involvement of genetic variation in the oxytocin receptor gene (OXTR) in the etiology of autistic disorders on high-functioning level. *American Journal of Medical Genetics Part B: Neuropsychiatric Genetics, 153B*(2), 629–639. doi:10.1002/ajmg.b.31032

Wetherby, A. M., Brosnan-Maddox, S., Peace, V., & Newton, L. (2008). Validation of the Infant—Toddler Checklist as a broadband screener for autism spectrum disorders from 9 to 24 months of age. *Autism, 12,* 487–511. doi:10.1177/1362361308094501

Wetherby, A. M., & Prizant, B. M. (2002). *Communication and Symbolic Behavior Scales: Developmental profile*. Baltimore, MD: Brookes.

Whalen, C., & Schreibman, L. (2003). Joint attention training for children with autism using behavior modification procedures. *Journal of Child Psychology and Psychiatry, 44*, 456–468. doi:10.1111/1469-7610.00135

White, S. W., Albano, A. M., Johnson, C. R., Kasari, C., Ollendick, T., Klin, A., . . . Scahill, L. (2010). Development of a cognitive-behavioral intervention program to treat anxiety and social deficits in teens with high-functioning autism. *Clinical Child and Family Psychology Review, 13*(1), 77–90. doi:10.1007/s10567-009-0062-3

White, S. W., Oswald, D., Ollendick, T., & Scahill, L. (2009). Anxiety in children and adolescents with autism spectrum disorders. *Clinical Psychology Review, 29*, 216–229. doi:10.1016/j.cpr.2009.01.003

Whitehouse, A. J. O., Durkin, K., Jaquet, E., & Ziatas, K. (2009). Friendship, loneliness and depression in adolescents with Asperger's syndrome. *Journal of Adolescence, 32*, 309–322. doi:10.1016/j.adolescence.2008.03.004

Whittingham, K., Sofronoff, K., Sheffield, J., & Sanders, M. R. (2009). Do parental attributions affect treatment outcome in a parenting program? An exploration of the effects of parental attributions in an RCT of Stepping Stones Triple P for the ASD population. *Research in Autism Spectrum Disorders, 3*, 129–144. doi:10.1016/j.rasd.2008.05.002

Wilczynski, S. M., Rue, H. C., Hunter, M., & Christian, L. (2012). Elementary behavioral intervention strategies: Discrete trial instruction, differential reinforcement, and shaping. In P. A. Prelock & R. J. McCauley (Eds.), *Treatment of autism spectrum disorders: Evidence based-intervention strategies for communication and social interactions* (pp. 49–77). Baltimore, MD: Brookes.

Williams, J., Allison, C., Scott, F., Stott, C., Bolton, P., Baron-Cohen, S., & Brayne, C. (2006). The Childhood Asperger Syndrome Test (CAST): Test–retest reliability. *Autism, 10*, 415–427. doi:10.1177/1362361306066612

Wing, L. (1980). Childhood autism and social class: A question of selection? *The British Journal of Psychiatry, 137*, 410–417. doi:10.1192/bjp.137.5.410

Wing, L., Gould, J., & Gillberg, C. (2011). Autism spectrum disorders in the DSM–V: Better or worse than the DSM–IV? *Research in Developmental Disabilities, 32*, 768–773. doi:10.1016/j.ridd.2010.11.003

Wing, L., Leekam, S. R., Libby, S. J., Gould, J., & Larcombe, M. (2002). The diagnostic interview for social and communication disorders: Background, interrater reliability and clinical use. *Journal of Child Psychology and Psychiatry, and Allied Disciplines, 43*, 307–325. doi:10.1111/1469-7610.00023

Wolff, J. J., Gu, H., Gerig, G., Elison, J. T., Styner, M., Gouttard, S., . . . Piven, J. (2012). Differences in white matter fiber tract development present from 6 to 24 months in infants with autism. *The American Journal of Psychiatry, 169,* 589–600. doi:10.1176/appi.ajp.2011.11091447

Wong, C., & Kasari, C. (2012). Play and joint attention of children with autism in the preschool special education classroom. *Journal of Autism and Developmental Disorders, 42,* 2152–2161.

Wood, J. J., Drahota, A., Sze, K., Har, K., Chiu, A., & Langer, D. A. (2009). Cognitive behavioral therapy for anxiety in children with autism spectrum disorders: A randomized, controlled trial. *Journal of Child Psychology and Psychiatry, 50,* 224–234. doi:10.1111/j.1469-7610.2008.01948.x

World Health Organization. (1993). *The ICD-10 classification of mental and behavioural disorders: Diagnostic criteria for research.* Geneva, Switzerland: Author.

Yama, B., Freeman, T., Graves, E., Yuan, S., & Campbell, M. (2012). Examination of the properties of the Modified Checklist for Autism in Toddlers (M-CHAT) in a population sample. *Journal of Autism and Developmental Disorders, 42*(1), 23–34. doi:10.1007/s10803-011-1211-3

Yoder, K. J., & Belmonte, M. K. (2011). Information processing and integration. In D. G. Amaral, G. Dawson, & D. Geschwind (Eds.), *Autism spectrum disorders* (pp. 1010–1027). New York, NY: Oxford University Press. doi:10.1093/med/9780195371826.003.0064

Zerbo, O., Iosif, A.-M., Walker, C., Ozonoff, S., Hansen, R., & Hertz-Picciotto, I. (2013). Is maternal influenza or fever during pregnancy associated with autism or developmental delays? Results from the CHARGE (Childhood autism risks from genetics and environment) study. *Journal of Autism and Developmental Disorders, 43,* 25–33. doi:10.1007/s10803-012-1540-x

Zona, M. L., Christodulu, K. V., & Durand, V. M. (2004, October). *Providing social support for siblings of children with autism: An evaluation of the SibShop model.* Poster presented at the 9th Annual Center for School Mental Health Assistance Conference on Advancing School-Based Mental Health, Dallas, TX.

Zwaigenbaum, L. (2011). Screening, risk, and early identification of autism spectrum disorders. In D. G. Amaral, G. Dawson, & D. Geschwind (Eds.), *Autism spectrum disorders* (pp. 75–89). New York, NY: Oxford University Press.

Index

About the Author

V. **Mark Durand, PhD,** is known worldwide as an authority in the area of autism spectrum disorder. He is a professor of psychology at the University of South Florida St. Petersburg (USFSP), where he was the founding dean of arts and sciences and vice chancellor for academic affairs. He was awarded the University Award for Excellence in Teaching at University at Albany, State University of New York in 1991 and in 2007 was given the Chancellor's Award for Excellence in Research and Creative Scholarship at the USFSP. Dr. Durand is currently a member of the Professional Advisory Board for the Autism Society of America and a fellow of the American Psychological Association. He is the coeditor of the *Journal of Positive Behavior Interventions* and has written more than 100 research publications and 10 books, including abnormal psychology textbooks that are used at more than 1,000 universities worldwide.

Major themes in Dr. Durand's research include the assessment and treatment of severe behavior problems for children and adults with autism, parent training, and the development of treatments for child sleep problems. He developed one of the most popular functional behavioral assessment instruments used today, the Motivation Assessment Scale, which has been translated into 15 languages. Recently, he developed an innovative approach to help families work with their challenging children and published a guide for parents and caregivers of children with autism spectrum disorder, *Optimistic Parenting: Hope and Help for You and Your Challenging Child,* which has won several national awards.